DOES MY CHILD HAVE AUTISM?

DOES MY CHILD HAVE AUTISM?

A Parent's Guide to Early Detection and Intervention in Autism Spectrum Disorders

Wendy L. Stone, Ph.D.

with Theresa Foy DiGeronimo, M.Ed.

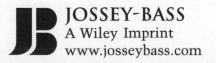

JOSSEY-BASS
A Wiley Imprint
www.josseybass.com

Published by Jossey-Bass
A Wiley Imprint
989 Market Street, San Francisco, CA 94103-1741   www.josseybass.com

Library of Congress Cataloging-in-Publication Data

Stone, Wendy L., date.
  Does my child have autism? : a parent's guide to early detection and intervention in autism spectrum disorders / Wendy L. Stone, Theresa Foy DiGeronimo.— 1st ed.
      p. cm.
    Includes bibliographical references and index.
    ISBN-13: 978-0-7879-8450-2 (pbk.)
    ISBN-10: 0-7879-8450-7 (pbk.)
  1. Autism in children—Diagnosis—Popular works.   2. Autistic children—Family relationships—Popular works.   3. Parents of autistic children—Popular works.   I. DiGeronimo, Theresa Foy.   II. Title.
    RJ506.A9.S767 2006
    618.92'85882—dc22   2005034988

Printed in the United States of America
FIRST EDITION
PB Printing   10 9 8 7 6 5 4 3 2 1

This book is dedicated to the memory of my parents,
Shirley Katz Stone and Leonard Stone,
whose passion for learning and capacity for loving
enabled me to follow the stars and find my path.
W.L.S.

CONTENTS

PREFACE

This is a book for parents—especially those who are concerned, worried, and confused. It is for those whose sleep is disturbed by the nagging question: "Does my child have autism?" It is for parents who think there might be a small chance, just maybe a possibility that their child is not developing as he or she should. It is also for those parents who see distinct signs of delay but aren't sure if they necessarily point to autism. And it is for those who have read about Autism Spectrum Disorders, have observed their child, and now believe that it is very likely that their child has autism. At whatever stage you may be in this process of discovery, I've written this book keeping in mind how you might be feeling. I have met and worked with many parents just like you.

I have dedicated the last twenty-five years of my life to children with autism and their parents through my clinical work and research. I'm a child psychologist and a scientist. I am also a parent. I know that gut-wrenching feeling that comes with the mere thought that something might be wrong with your child. And I know how hard it is for you to ask tough questions when you don't really want to hear the answers, so I admire your willingness to do what's best for your child, no matter how hard it is for you.

The purpose of this book is to give you straightforward, up-to-date, and scientifically sound information. The chapters are organized according to the sequence of events you will most likely follow as you move forward in your quest to better understand your child's behavior. The book opens with a general discussion of Autism Spectrum Disorders, so that you clearly understand how the medical community defines these disorders and distinguishes them from each other. Chapter Two then explains very specific behaviors that are commonly seen in children with autism that you can look for in your child. Chapter Three takes you step-by-step through the diagnostic process for young children with autism so that you'll understand what to expect—and what will be expected of you and your child—during this process. In Chapter Four, you'll learn why early intervention for children with autism is so vitally important and about the different types of interventions that are available. In Chapter Five, I'll give you some tips, activities, and teaching tools that you can use at home to improve your child's social, communication, and play skills.

Although I understand that your mind and heart may get wrapped up in the signs and symptoms of autism during this uncertain period, it's so very important never to lose sight of one unchangeable fact: kids are kids whether or not they have the diagnosis of autism. The diagnosis gives you and your child's health care and education professionals the information needed to help your child reach his or her full potential, but the diagnosis does not change who he or she is today. Your child is the same as he or she was before the diagnosis—a child who, like all children, needs your love and support and acceptance. It is my hope that this book will give you the facts you need in order to know your child better so that you can enjoy each other, learn from each other, and appreciate the unique joy and magic that he or she brings to your family.

Acknowledgments

I would like to acknowledge with deep gratitude the many families with whom I have interacted and from whom I have learned so much. In a way, I will be sharing all of their stories so that we can help others who are traveling a similar path.

I would also like to acknowledge the contributions of many people who have helped me formulate and develop ideas that are expressed in this book. Over the years there have been numerous teachers, supervisors, colleagues, graduate students, and TRIAD clinicians who have shared their experiences and insights with me. I am grateful for the opportunities we have had to exchange ideas and grow together in our knowledge and understanding of autism.

Words cannot come close to expressing the appreciation I feel for my husband and son, who have remained patient and understanding as I have disappeared into my computer to write this book. Their gracious and forgiving spirits have been a source of inspiration as well as support, and I hope they know how often I marvel at my fortune in being able to share my life with them.

Finally, I would like to thank my editor, Alan Rinzler, without whose vision this book would not have been written, and whose encouragement and enthusiasm created a true partnership.

Wendy L. Stone
Nashville, Tennessee

DOES MY CHILD HAVE AUTISM?

1

WHAT EXACTLY ARE AUTISM SPECTRUM DISORDERS?

What's going on? Why is the word *autism*—virtually unheard of in your parents' generation—now audible everywhere you turn? It seems as if every family has some concern or connection with autism these days—and there's no avoiding it. In the past year, autism was the subject of 116 articles in the *New York Times*. Do a search on Google and you'll discover over five million hits. Amazon.com offers 1,076 books on the subject. Given this autism overload, no wonder you may feel a sense of dread when you call your child's name and he or she is slow to respond!

Yet despite the publicity that has surrounded this disorder in the last few years, few people know what autism really is. And because a little knowledge can truly be a dangerous thing, the word has become misused and misunderstood—it's become entangled in a web of disorders with similar, often overlapping ranges of symptoms. And because the symptoms of classic autism itself can be present in different combinations and at different levels of severity, the question of whether or not your child has autism—or where your child's behavior fits within the range of possible autistic symptoms—has become very confusing.

The fact is that autism is one type of developmental disorder within a range of what are called Autism Spectrum Disorders. Autism Spectrum Disorders include Autistic Disorder, Asperger's

Disorder, Rett's Disorder, Childhood Disintegrative Disorder, and Pervasive Developmental Disorder Not Otherwise Specified (PDDNOS). Children within the range of Autism Spectrum Disorders show impairments across a number of developmental areas, including difficulty with social interactions, disordered language development, and repetitive activities and behaviors. These symptoms overlap not only from one autism spectrum disorder to another, but also with other nonautistic developmental disorders such as language delay or global developmental delay. This is why it's often difficult for health care professionals* to diagnose autism quickly—and why it is so intolerably frustrating for parents who think they see symptoms that might spell trouble—but might not—and can't get a quick and clear answer.

With other childhood illnesses, we're accustomed to familiar and conventional symptoms and rapid diagnosis. Is your baby crying, suffering a slight fever, and tugging on his ear? A medical evaluation is likely to show signs of an ear infection (*otitis media*) that's treated with a ten-day course of antibiotics. Symptoms, signs, diagnosis, treatment—done. But along come symptoms that the television and print media, family, and friends say look like autism, and suddenly no one can quickly and definitively answer your questions. It's ambiguous; it's hard to pin down; it's alarming.

HOW THIS BOOK CAN HELP YOU

I understand your distress and confusion. I'm a mother. I'm also a psychologist who has worked with hundreds of families who have children with Autism Spectrum Disorders. I have made it my life's work to come up with the information that will help you map your way through the jargon, complexities, and frustration of autism. I

---

*The term *health care professional* refers to professionals who diagnose and treat mental health or physical health conditions. The diagnosis of autism is most commonly made by clinical psychologists, psychiatrists, and developmental pediatricians.

know that you wouldn't be reading this book if you didn't already have concerns about your child's development, so I have written it to speak directly to you. I imagine sitting with you in the clinic, seeing the worry in your eyes as you ask, "Does my child have autism?" And I understand that you would want an accurate and quick yes-or-no answer. After all, you realize that the sooner you can have a firm diagnosis, the better for your child. And that explains that sense of urgency I hear in your voice.

If you really were sitting here with me, I would be the first to agree that early detection and intervention are so very important for your child. But before I could answer your question, we would both need to gather the facts and then carefully put all the pieces together. And that's exactly what we'll do through the chapters of this book.

In this first chapter, we discuss the signs and symptoms of the Autism Spectrum Disorders. Before you move on to any other chapter, please read this information carefully and then heed this advice: don't jump to conclusions if you see evidence of some of the symptoms in your child. There are many children, for example, who do not speak the expected fifty words by the age of two, yet do not have autism. So wait to get all the facts before you make yourself crazy with worry.

Let's take this exploration of autism one small step at a time. In this first chapter, take time to gain a better understanding of Autism Spectrum Disorders *in general*. This is the foundation you need *before* you can observe and evaluate your own child using the guidelines given in Chapter Two. Then with the Chapter Two checklist in hand, you can share your concerns and observations with your child's pediatrician.

If you and the pediatrician decide that an evaluation is warranted, you can refer to Chapter Three for some guidelines for what to expect during this process. Then, if necessary, you can move on to Chapters Four and Five regarding appropriate interventions and education. Please try to be patient; jumping ahead or to conclusions won't lead you to the information you need to help your child.

⚏ By the Numbers

The number of children diagnosed with autism has increased dramatically over the past ten years, making it the fastest-growing developmental disability in the nation. In fact, the Centers for Disease Control and Prevention has found that autism now affects an estimated 1 in 250 births, and that this diagnosis is growing at a rate of 10 to 17 percent each year. At this rate, the Autism Society of America estimates that autism could affect four million Americans in the next decade.[1] The reasons for this increase are complex and include better recognition, earlier diagnosis, and more inclusive diagnostic criteria.

THE MYTH VERSUS THE REALITY

You've probably heard through the media or in discussions with other parents that children with autism live in a world of their own, are unresponsive to their environment, and make odd, repetitive movements, such as rocking or flapping their arms. This is sometimes true—but not necessarily. TV news reports and special programs almost always show the most severe cases; those children make for "good" programming.

I saw this firsthand when a TV crew came to film some children with autism at the TRIAD clinic at Vanderbilt Kennedy Center and Vanderbilt Children's Hospital in Nashville, Tennessee. The children were well behaved despite the presence of so many extra adults in the room and lots of equipment, including hot, bright lights for the camera. I was delighted that we'd be able to show viewers images of children with autism who played with toys or sat at a table to work, rather than spent their time making odd noises or engaging in repetitive actions. But the producer of the show was not so happy. She kept insisting that her reporter get more footage of children who were demonstrating the most unusual behaviors, and she kept directing the cameraman to focus exclusively on those with the most extreme symptoms—not on the majority of children who were calm and well behaved. Clearly, some members of the media do not want to see children with autism who look just fine.

This need to focus on only the sensational side of a story perpetuates one of the myths surrounding the fear of autism—that these children are entirely nonfunctioning. This is not true. Children with autism can vary tremendously from one another in the way they show the symptoms of this disorder, and that's why such vague terms as *autistic-like*, *autistic tendencies*, and *high-functioning* or *low-functioning autism* are sometimes used to differentiate the symptoms of one child from those of another.

In truth, if you had the opportunity to view a room of young children with autism, you would see some children talking and others using pictures or sign language to communicate. Some children would be sitting with their peers, others sitting by themselves. Some would be working at a table, others running back and forth along a wall or climbing on furniture. Some might be laughing during a tickle game with their parents, others having a tantrum and throwing toys. Looking at this group, you would wonder, "Which of these children have autism?" The simple answer is that they all do.

UNDERSTANDING THE DIFFERENT AUTISM SPECTRUM DISORDERS

The description of children with autism gets confusing because sometimes people use different terms to refer to the same thing, and sometimes they use the same term to refer to different things. The *Diagnostic and Statistical Manual of Mental Disorders, Fourth Edition (DSM-IV)* is the book that health care professionals use to describe the characteristics necessary for the diagnosis of specific mental health, behavioral, and developmental disorders. The *DSM-IV* has established the umbrella term *Pervasive Developmental Disorders (PDD)* to include autism and four other related disorders that share signs and symptoms. In other words, the terms *Autism Spectrum*

:♡: PARENTS SAY
What Autism "Looks" Like

- My son is a beautiful boy; you'd never guess he has any issues just by looking at him. Autism isn't always something that can be noticed by outward appearance, so when he begins to melt down in public, people act as if he's an undisciplined nuisance, and they treat me as if I'm a bad parent. (mother of three-year-old boy)
- Most people don't know how broad the autism spectrum is. They assume autism is much more severe than it is in our son (think Rain Man) and often suspect that we are hypochondriac parents since our son is high functioning. My sister gasped in horror when I first told her about my son's diagnosis—I guess she thought he was somehow doomed to live in an institution or something. (mother of five-year-old boy diagnosed at age two)
- Movie and television characters with autism tend to be on the severe side. I know that only trouble is interesting, but it does my son no good to portray autism as something akin to severe retardation or freakishness. And it tends to keep parents of newly diagnosed children from overcoming their sense of denial. (mother of five-year-old boy)

Disorders and *Pervasive Developmental Disorders* are often used to mean the same thing. Both terms refer to a class of disorders that includes social deficits, communication impairments, and restricted, repetitive activities as their primary characteristics. **For the purpose of this book, I will use the term *Autism Spectrum Disorders* (or ASDs) to refer to autism and related disorders that share the core features,** and the term *Pervasive Developmental Disorders* (or PDDs) only when describing specific *DSM-IV* categories or diagnostic criteria.

The five disorders categorized as Pervasive Developmental Disorders in *DSM-IV* are (1) Autistic Disorder, (2) Asperger's Disorder, (3) Rett's Disorder, (4) Childhood Disintegrative Disorder, and (5) Pervasive Developmental Disorder Not Otherwise Specified (PDDNOS). These disorders differ from each other on features that include their prevalence, severity, and the way in which their symptoms appear and progress.

As you begin your exploration of autism, it's important to take some time to become familiar with each of the five Pervasive Developmental Disorders. So let's go through them briefly.

Autistic Disorder

Autistic Disorder is the formal term for what is more commonly called "autism." This disorder is characterized by a pattern of severe impairments in three areas: (1) difficulties interacting with others in a reciprocal way, (2) impaired language and communication skills, and (3) a repetitive and restricted range of interests and activities. (See Appendix A for specific *DSM-IV* criteria for Autistic Disorder.) These symptoms emerge before the age of three, but can change over time and vary widely from one child to another. (We'll be looking at each symptom more fully later in the chapter.) For reasons that are unclear at this time, boys are more likely to be diagnosed with Autistic Disorder by a ratio of approximately 4:1.

Asperger's Disorder

The name "Asperger" comes from Hans Asperger, an Austrian physician who first described the disorder in 1944. This PDD describes children (predominantly boys by a 5:1 ratio) who have average intelligence and who do not have a history of delayed language development. They do, however, have social impairments and restricted, repetitive interests. Their social interactions can be awkward and one-sided, and they often have difficulty understanding the perspectives of others. They may talk unceasingly about some object or topic of fascination, not understanding the give-and-take of conversation or the art of listening.

This diagnosis is used only when the impairments are severe and sustained and interfere with the child's functioning at home, school, or in the community. Many times the symptoms of Asperger's are not evident until the child begins school, which is why this diagnosis is not often made in children under age three.

Rett's Disorder

Named for Dr. Andreas Rett, an Austrian physician who first described the disorder in a journal article in 1966, Rett's Disorder is very rare, affecting girls almost exclusively. Children with this disorder develop normally and on schedule through early infancy. But then sometime between six and eighteen months, they gradually begin to lose skills in different areas of functioning. Children who had been talking, stop. Their ability to interact with others decreases. They also lose the use of their hands to hold and manipulate objects and begin to show repetitive hand movements such as hand rubbing, clasping, or wringing. During this phase of their regression, they show symptoms similar to those seen in Autistic Disorder.

The symptoms of Rett's Disorder are progressive and worsen over time. Rett's Disorder is the only PDD that has an identified genetic cause: an abnormality of a gene on the X chromosome.

Childhood Disintegrative Disorder (CDD)

CDD is a very rare condition that involves a significant regression in skills in children who have had typical development for the first two years of life. (This lengthy period of typical development is a key difference between Rett's Disorder and CDD.) Between the ages of two and ten, children with CDD lose some or all of the skills they have already developed in areas that include language, social skills, play, and motor skills. Following this period of regression, their behavior stabilizes (also unlike Rett's Disorder), though children usually have severe mental retardation and may also have seizures.

Pervasive Developmental Disorder Not Otherwise Specified (PDDNOS)

PDDNOS is what's called a "diagnosis of exclusion." It is used only when a child demonstrates symptoms of PDD that do not fit the criteria specified for one of the other disorders in this category. Specifically, the diagnosis of PDDNOS is used for children who are impaired in their social interactions along with *either* an impairment in the development of language and communication skills *or* a pattern of restricted or repetitive behaviors and activities.

For example, a child may receive a diagnosis of PDDNOS rather than Autistic Disorder if he or she does not show all the symptoms required for a diagnosis of Autistic Disorder or if his or her symptoms are milder in nature. The diagnostic criteria used for PDDNOS are less exact than those for the other diagnostic classifications within the category of PDD.

❧

I'm sure that the differences between each PDD are now clear as mud to you. For further clarification, you can refer to Table 1.1, but surely you will still wonder, "So what does all this have to do with autism?" and "How can I tell if my child has autism and not one of the other PDDs?" Keep reading!

FOCUSING ON AUTISTIC DISORDER AND PDDNOS

To simplify the answers to those questions, I am going to pull out two of the PDDs to focus on for the rest of this book: Autistic Disorder and PDDNOS. These are the disorders that are seen and diagnosed

TABLE 1.1. Characteristics of Pervasive Developmental Disorders.

Characteristic	Autistic Disorder	Asperger's Disorder	PDDNOS	Childhood Disintegrative Disorder	Rett's Disorder
Social impairment	X	X	X	X[b]	X
Language and communication disorder	X		X[a]	X[b]	X
Repetitive interests and activities	X	X	X[a]	X[b]	
Average intelligence		X			
Onset prior to 36 months	X				X
Period of normal development followed by loss of skills in several areas				X	X
Relative impairment	Variable	Milder	Milder	More severe	More severe
Relative prevalence	Higher	Intermediate	Higher	Lower	Lower

Note: [a]At least one of these two features must be present.
[b]At least two of these three features must be present.

most commonly in children under three, and are therefore most relevant to you and your young child as you look for the keys to early detection and intervention. Rett's Disorder and Childhood Disintegrative Disorder are quite rare and are very different in course and outcome from Autistic Disorder and PDDNOS. Asperger's Disorder is rarely detected before the age of three, and it does not present the very worrisome early symptoms that send parents rushing to their child's pediatrician for answers. If you are wondering if your child under the age of three has symptoms of autism, Asperger's is unlikely to be the diagnosis.

The differences between Autistic Disorder and PDDNOS can be quite subtle and often difficult to determine in young children. Compared to children diagnosed with Autistic Disorder, children with PDDNOS typically have milder symptoms, atypical symptoms, or both. Still, one health care professional might determine that a young child has PDDNOS, whereas another, who is equally competent, might determine that the same child has Autistic Disorder. **For the purpose of this book, which is focused on the young child, I will use the term *autism* to refer to both Autistic Disorder and PDDNOS.**

COMMON SYMPTOMS OF AUTISM

As indicated previously, there can be a lot of variability in the way that autism is expressed from one child to another. Here's why:

1. No two children are alike, whether they have autism or not. In the same way, each child with autism is an individual, with his or her own personality and unique characteristics.

2. Each child with autism displays a range of behaviors, some of which look just like what we expect for his or her age and some of which are different—or unusual—compared to other children. This behavioral variability is exactly what makes autism hard to identify in young children.

But whatever the range, intensity, or frequency of symptoms, they will include atypical development in these three primary areas: (1) social skills, (2) language and communication skills, and (3) repetitive and restricted behaviors. Although the symptoms in each area can vary from one child with autism to the next, let's take a look at what is typically found in these children.

Symptom 1: Impaired Social Skills

Humans instinctively interact with each other. Even in infancy, babies are interested in faces; they like close physical contact with caregivers; they turn toward voices and smile with recognition at familiar family members. As they grow, babies learn how to be social and interactive by watching how others talk, play, and relate with each other. They enjoy the give-and-take of social engagement and will initiate, maintain, and respond to interactions with others. In fact, they seek out those interactions.

Children with autism, however, often do not show the expected development of early social interaction skills. They seem not to have the same "drive" to interact socially as their peers do. In fact, impaired social interactions are the hallmark of autism and are present in *all* children with this diagnosis. ***If your child does not have difficulty initiating or responding to interactions with others, then your child does not have autism.***

These social impairments affect children's interactions with adults as well as with other children. They affect children's ability to initiate interactions with others as well as to respond to interactions that are initiated by others. For example, unlike other children, children with autism *may not*

- Pay attention to adults, even when they are close by
- Smile in response to praise or an adult's smile
- Respond when an adult calls their name
- Initiate social interactions with adults or peers

- Show enjoyment in interactive or turn-taking games with adults, such as patty-cake or peek-a-boo
- Imitate actions of adults, such as waving good-bye
- Repeat actions that adults respond to with praise or attention
- Show interest in other children, such as watching them or playing near them
- Join another child in play
- Play interactive, back-and-forth games with other children
- Show an interest in making friends
- Imitate the actions of other children
- Initiate play with other children, such as greeting them or handing them a toy

Each of these symptoms of social impairment may vary in frequency and intensity from one child with autism to another, but social deficits are an important marker of the disorder.

Symptom 2: Impaired Language and Communication Skills

Problems with language and communication can take many forms in children with autism. To understand these symptoms better, you need to understand the difference between communication, language, and speech:

Communication is a *process* through which someone conveys a message to another person. Communication can be verbal, which involves using words, or nonverbal, which involves using other behaviors, such as crying, reaching, gesturing, or facial expressions. In contrast, *language* refers to a *system* of communication in which conventional symbols are used to convey a message. Examples of conventional symbols are sign language, gestures, and words. Crying is not a symbol, nor is pulling on an adult's hand. *Speech* refers specifically to a *form* of language in which spoken words are used to communicate.

The most commonly recognized characteristic of autism in the domain of language and communication is the delayed development of spoken language. Nearly all children with autism are delayed in reaching their language milestones (see "Language Development Milestones" in Chapter Two). But the problems often go deeper than just language. Many children with autism do not understand the process of communication at all—they don't seem to know that there is a way for them to convey their needs and desires to other people. They don't know how to ask for help or ask for more or make a choice, other than by fussing or crying. Of course this deficit is terribly frustrating for parents—but imagine how frustrating it must be for the child!

Similar to their impairments in the social domain, children with autism have difficulty initiating communication as well as responding to the communication of others. For example, unlike other children with typical language and communication skills, children with autism *may not*

- Look at people in the eye during playful interactions
- Follow another person's point by looking in the direction indicated
- Express their needs or desires to others in conventional ways, such as reaching and vocalizing
- Use nonverbal gestures, such as waving good-bye or nodding or shaking their head
- Look at other people's faces to seek information
- Communicate for the purpose of sharing their interests or achievements with others, such as pointing to objects or holding them up to show to others
- Engage in back-and-forth babble "conversations"

Even children with autism who eventually develop spoken language still have impairments in this area. Like many children learning to speak, they may echo back words and phrases they hear. But unlike other children, those with autism may mimic the exact intonation of the speaker and persist in this echoing (called echolalia) long after other children have moved on to interactive speech, usually by three years of age.

Sometimes children with autism echo words or phrases they have just heard; this is called immediate echolalia. An example is a child's answering the question, "Do you want to go outside?" with "Go outside." Another type of echolalia occurs when children repeat things they have heard in another context (delayed echolalia). Examples of delayed echolalia occur when children repeat dialogue from videotapes or things that they have heard their teacher say at school. One of the most baffling things about autism is that some children can repeat long segments from favorite videotapes or books, but cannot use words functionally, to achieve their goals, such as by requesting a cookie or favorite snack.

Symptom 3: Restricted Interests and Repetitive Activities

Some children with autism become preoccupied with a particular activity, toy, or interest in a way that is unusual in its intensity. They may, for example, spend hours opening and closing the door on a toy car. Or they may line up puzzle pieces over and over again— never actually putting them into the puzzle.

These children may also find comfort and security in repetition of certain routines, patterns, or rituals. They may insist on following a certain pattern during dressing: socks first, pants next, then shirt, and so on. They may need to have the same plate and cup during mealtime. Sometimes, if their set routine is changed, they will explode in a temper tantrum of frustration.

Young children with autism may also show unusual repetitive movements that seem to serve no particular function. For example, some children may repeatedly flap their hands, flick their fingers, or spin around in a circle. Much more rarely, they may show self-injurious behaviors such as banging their heads or biting their hands.

Some children with autism also demonstrate unusual sensory responses, which may vary widely from child to child. For example, some children enjoy rubbing certain surfaces or are hypersensitive to the feel of new clothes. Many children avoid foods that have certain textures (though we certainly see picky eating habits in young children without autism as well!). Some children are very attentive to small details, such as a piece of thread on the floor, yet stumble over large objects in their paths. Some children appear distressed when they hear certain sounds, such as a vacuum cleaner or hair dryer, yet do not respond when a parent calls their name.

Despite the variation in the types and extent of restricted interests and repetitive activities, some examples of behaviors that may be observed are

- Engaging in repetitive play activities, such as lining up toys or spinning objects
- Acting out repetitive movements, such as running in circles or flicking their fingers
- Showing prolonged visual interest in objects, such as flapping objects in front of their eyes or staring at mirrors or objects that spin
- Having overly focused interest in one object or activity, such as a fascination with boats or bugs
- Demanding rigid adherence to rituals and routines
- Focusing attention on small parts of toys, such as the wheels on a toy truck, rather than the whole

Repetitive activities often go hand in hand with impaired play skills. Around the age of eighteen months, most children will flex their imaginations by turning a banana into a telephone, a bowl into a hat, or a clothespin into a little man. Because young children with autism often have very literal thinking patterns, they may not be able to see that a stick is anything more than a stick—not a sword, plane, or totem pole, as other children may imagine. They may not pretend that their teddy bear is injured and in need of a hug.

With respect to play skills, children with autism *may not*

- Play with a variety of toys
- Use toys the way they're designed to be used (such as stirring a spoon in a bowl)
- Arrange toys in their intended scheme (such as placing toy dishes on a table)
- Show functional play with dolls, stuffed animals, or toy figures (such as feeding a doll or putting a toy figure in a car for a ride)
- Create play sequences (such as putting the little people on the toy bus, driving the bus to its pretend destination, and then taking all the little people out of the bus)
- Play with toys in a variety of ways (such as pushing a toy car back and forth as well as filling the car with gas, driving it around, rolling it down a hill)

❧

Early problems related to the development of social skills, language and communication skills, and restricted and repetitive interests and activities are the primary symptoms used to diagnose autism. Exactly how you and your child's health care professional should evaluate these developmental problems is explained in later chapters. For now, in this early step, be sure you have a clear understanding of how these three symptoms show themselves *in general* among children with autism.

Because the symptoms in each of the three domains that characterize autism can vary so widely from one child to the next, it's far too early in your exploration of autism to make any assumptions about your own child. You'll see in Table 1.2 examples of how autism can show itself in different ways.

TABLE 1.2. Variability in Symptom Expression: Three Two-Year-Olds with Autism.

Jacob	Will	Amy
	Social Behaviors	
• Is very attached to his mother; likes to be in the same room with her; will climb up on her lap to twirl her hair or pat her cheek; is very clingy to her in new situations	• Mostly stays to himself; can occupy himself for hours on end; doesn't seek out parents as play partners	• Is very active and happy; likes to run around the house; will tolerate her parents' presence as long as they don't try to get her to do things
• Is less responsive to his father, but has a favorite game in which he climbs up his father's legs to be flipped over	• Shows little interest in his baby brother or older sister; gets upset when the baby cries; will occasionally play a chase game with his sister	• Can sit and watch videotapes for hours, but does not sit at the table during mealtimes for more than a few minutes at a time
• Shows little interest in other children; sometimes watches them, but keeps his distance	• Becomes upset in new places or when approached by adults other than his parents; does not like to be held and is not easily calmed when upset	• Likes to go to the park and run around; does not pay attention to the other children, even when they try to get her to play

Communication Behaviors

- Constantly jabbers, but is hard to understand; vocalizations seem to be more for his own entertainment than a way to communicate; sometimes seems to be acting out scenes from videotapes
- Every now and then will say a new word, but does not use any words consistently

- Is very quiet; rarely makes any sounds at all, other than humming or crying
- Cries when he wants something, but does not indicate what he wants by pointing or reaching; parents have to guess what he wants by offering him different objects; will push away things he doesn't want

- Usually tries to get things herself rather than ask for help; will climb on tables and chairs to reach things
- Sometimes will pull a parent by the hand to the kitchen when hungry or to the door to go outside
- Learned the alphabet by eighteen months; will call out letters when she sees them, but does not use words

Restricted and Repetitive Behaviors

- Likes to watch certain videos; can independently get the tape he wants and operate the VCR
- Will watch the same video for several weeks at a time; covers his ears and runs out of the room during certain parts; will replay the credits over and over
- Becomes very upset if he is not able to watch the complete tape

- Favorite toys are cars and any vehicles with wheels
- Likes to line up cars and arrange them on the floor and in shoe boxes; becomes very upset if his sister tries to play along with him or disturbs his arrangement
- Often lies on the floor to watch the wheels as he rolls the cars near his eyes

- Doesn't play with any of her toys; prefers household objects instead
- Favorite activities are to line up and sort forks and spoons and to roll soda bottles back and forth across the floor
- Always has to have a fork or spoon in her hand; will sometimes hold it up close to her eyes to examine it or flip it in front of her face

THE CAUSE OF AUTISM

The only honest answer that I can give to the question "What causes autism?" is this: no one knows for sure. This is a very unsatisfying response, I know, but it's the best any of us in the field can come up with at this time.

I've seen the books that dedicate entire chapters to the exploration of a cause. Perhaps, they say, it is caused by fragile X syndrome or phenylketonuria or neurofibromatosis; or it may be caused by viral infections, such as congenital rubella, cytomegalovirus, or herpes encephalitis; or maybe it's due to metabolic conditions, such as abnormalities of purine synthesis or carbohydrate metabolism; it might go back to problems during pregnancy; or it may be caused by the child's immune system or sensitivity to certain foods; and of course we've all heard the possibility that there is a link between autism and the use of thimerosal, a mercury-based preservative present in the measles-mumps-rubella (MMR) vaccine. (Although mercury is no longer used in childhood vaccines in the United States and many large-scale studies have failed to show a link between thimerosal and autism, the theory persists.)

So what is the answer? We do know that autism affects the way the brain develops, because the brain is responsible for the functions that are impaired in autism. And we know that parents do not cause their child's autism. Scientists involved in autism research believe that there is no one single cause of autism that operates for all children. More than likely, we will find that there are different combinations of factors that can cause this disorder in different children—perhaps explaining why the symptoms differ so much from one child to the next.

Fortunately, the scientific community is now beginning to unlock some of the mysteries that surround autism. For example, we do know that genetic factors can increase a child's vulnerability or risk for having autism. This type of genetic influence is different from that seen in other disorders such as Down syndrome or cystic fibrosis, in which a genetic mutation actually causes the disorder.

Testing of twins has found that if one identical twin (twins from the same fertilized egg and therefore genetically identical) has autism, it is highly likely (better than a 50:50 chance) that the other twin will also have autism. If autism were purely genetic, the risk would be 100 percent. But autism does run in families. When one child in the family has autism, his or her siblings are more likely also to have autism compared to siblings in nonaffected families. However, scientists have not yet identified the specific combination of genes that act together to increase children's vulnerability to autism.

Many families will question how their child with autism could have inherited the disorder, when no one else in their extended family has autism. In these cases, it's not unusual to find that there are some family members who, upon close examination, do have some behaviors that are consistent with autism-like symptoms. For example, they may be socially awkward, may have had language delays as a child, may have highly restricted interests, or may have some combination of these. These symptoms are often milder than those seen in individuals diagnosed with autism and are referred to as the "broader autism phenotype." (A phenotype is the physical or behavioral expression of genes.)

The genetics of autism are complicated because the inherited vulnerability for autism may not result in behavioral symptoms of autism for all children. Scientists believe that a genetic tendency toward autism must operate in combination with other, noninherited factors—such as environmental influences—in order for a child to express the characteristic behaviors of autism.

For example, early environmental factors might include interruption of oxygen to the baby's brain during birth, the mother having German measles during the pregnancy, or even exposure to a pesticide. Each of these conditions may negatively influence brain development, but I have to emphasize that the exact combination of underlying genetic and environmental factors that causes autism is one of the large missing pieces in this complex puzzle.

Researchers have also determined that a child is not at increased risk for autism because of his or her racial, ethnic, geographical, or socioeconomic background. For unknown reasons, however, boys are three to four times more likely than girls to have autism. But keep in mind that males are at higher risk than females for many developmental problems, including Attention-Deficit/Hyperactivity Disorder and learning disabilities.

There are far more unknowns than knowns about the cause of autism at this time. I believe the discovery of the elusive cause (more likely, causes) will come only after a long and complex search that involves collaboration among researchers specializing in the biological, brain, and behavioral sciences.

THE IMPORTANCE OF EARLY DETECTION AND INTERVENTION

The cause of autism is not yet known, and there is no known cure at this time. But all is not hopeless. Research has identified many educational practices that are effective in helping children with autism improve their skills and behavior (see Chapter Four). The outcomes for children with autism who are diagnosed early and who receive specialized early intervention services are much better today than in the past—in terms of their cognitive development, language ability, social skills, and overall behavioral functioning. In fact, some children who receive a diagnosis of autism at age two no longer have the diagnosis two or three years later.

It's true! I used to tell parents of children with autism that their child would probably have the disorder for the rest of his or her life. But I no longer have to say that, now that we are diagnosing autism so much earlier, and intervening more effectively. If young children diagnosed with autism receive appropriate intervention, their path of development can be altered in very positive ways. Early intervention can change the way the brain develops in these children. The percentage of children with autism who "leave the spectrum" is still small, and we don't yet have a way to predict which children will leave their diagnosis behind, but research is underway to help answer this question.

RESEARCH TODAY

There has been a great deal of discussion and research on the possibility of a link between childhood vaccines and autism. The U.S. Centers for Disease Control and Prevention (CDC) conducts and supports many of the federal studies of large populations (epidemiological studies) that have closely examined this possibility. The most carefully conducted research on the connection between autism and vaccines has not found a link. For accurate and up-to-date information about this research, visit the following Web site: www.cdc.gov/nip/vacsafe/concerns/autism/default.htm.

You can also find out more about this issue from an article called "FAQs About MMR Vaccine and Autism," published by the National Immunization Program, at www.cdc.gov/nip/vacsafe/concerns/autism/autism-mmr.htm and from another called "Autism and the MMR Vaccine," published by the National Institute of Child Health and Human Development, at www.nichd.nih.gov/publications/pubs/autism/mmr/index.htm.

Knowing this, parents can focus on what their children need right now to help with their development; they can hold on to the hope that their child will be one of those who have every indication of autism at age two but then don't have it a few years later. Most often, the children who leave the autism spectrum still have some developmental issues, such as language impairments or developmental delays, but their behavioral improvements can be truly remarkable.

FREQUENTLY ASKED QUESTIONS

Here and at the end of each chapter, I answer some of the questions about autism that I am often asked by parents of young children.

Are there more children with autism today than in the past?

It's very hard to determine whether there are more children with autism now or whether we are just better at identifying and diagnosing the disorder. Although autism was first identified in 1943, it is very possible that many individuals with autism were misdiagnosed until the 1970s or even 1980s. The higher-functioning children who used language and had average cognitive skills may have gone through the regular education system in school and may have been considered "odd" by their classmates. Others may have been diagnosed with schizophrenia due to their unusual behavior. Children functioning at lower cognitive levels were likely to have been classified as having mental retardation rather than autism. There wasn't as much effort as now to distinguish between the subtleties among the various developmental disorders.

It is definitely the case that there are more children *diagnosed* with autism today than there were in years past. This is happening in part because there is greater awareness of the signs and symptoms of this disorder in the health care community (and among parents!), so now more children are getting the proper diagnosis. Also, we are now able to diagnose autism at a much younger age than we were in years past. Adding two- and three-year-olds to the number of older children with the diagnosis will naturally raise the total number.

Finally, the criteria for diagnosing autism have changed over time to be more inclusive. Children with milder impairments are now being identified, which also contributes to the larger numbers of children with the diagnosis. So . . . yes, the number of children *diagnosed* with autism has increased, but it's less clear whether the actual number of children with autism has changed dramatically over the years.

How do I know that my two-year-old child doesn't just have a speech delay?

This is an important question, because the methods used to treat delays in spoken language are not the same as those used for autism. There are two important ways that young children with autism differ from children with speech delays alone. First, children with speech delays (who don't have autism) are able to communicate with others—they just have difficulty using words to do so. They manage to figure out nonverbal ways of communicating their needs, likes, and dislikes, such as by pointing to things they want or wrinkling their noses to let their parents know what they *don't* like. In contrast, young children with autism typically have difficulty communicating both nonverbally and verbally.

Second, children with delays in spoken language do not show the impairments in social relating and reciprocity that children with autism do. They have more social interest and enjoy getting their parents' attention by acting silly to make them laugh or showing them a puzzle they have completed. Like other children without autism, they seek out interactions with others and enjoy the give-and-take of engaging with other people.

My wife and I have a five-year-old boy who has autism, and we just had our second child, a baby boy. How likely is it that our baby will have autism?

Because autism is a disorder in which increased risk can be inherited, your second child does have a greater chance of having autism than other children do—but the risk is still fairly low. The recurrence risk of autism for later-born siblings of children with autism ranges from 3 percent to 8 percent. That means that somewhere between three and eight children out of every hundred children born to families that already have a child with autism will receive a diagnosis of autism. Later-born siblings also have an increased risk of showing some features of autism (that is, the "broader phenotype") without demonstrating the full-blown disorder.

❧

Don't let the information in this introductory chapter scare you. It's intended to give you a solid understanding of the characteristics of autism and their many manifestations *in general*. This should help you separate the media hype from the facts and give you a base to stand on as you read the next chapter. It's time to turn the page and find out how to apply the facts about autism to your own young child.

2

WHAT SHOULD
I LOOK FOR?

Young children can be unpredictable—and strong-willed. That wonderful bye-bye wave they practice all day long disappears suddenly when you want to show it off to Grandma. The child who said "dada" unceasingly at lunchtime stares at you dumbfounded as you beg him to "say Daddy" when his father comes home for dinner. That's just the way children are. And that's why autism cannot be diagnosed during a brief visit with the child's doctor, especially in very young children.

Because we know that the behavior of young children can change from one moment to the next, health care professionals generally try to cut children some slack during office or clinic visits. We try not to judge them negatively on the basis of their behavior during a single short visit. If they're not being responsive to us, we tend to consider that maybe they're feeling cranky at that moment, or maybe they're just shy. If they don't smile at us or wave to us, it's possible that they're being typical of the many children who are wary of strangers and who just take a longer time to "warm up" to people. In these situations, we tend to assume that the children have the *ability* to interact and respond socially but just don't feel like doing it when we happen to be observing them.

Most of the time this assumption is probably correct. But when it comes to children with autism, it can be dangerous to assume that they have the capacity for better or more complete interactions.

What we consider to be "cutting them slack" may be more like ignoring a gigantic red flag that is staring us in the face.

So how do we know how to interpret the behaviors we observe? How can we tell whether the aloof child in front of us is just momentarily shy or cranky or whether this behavior commonly occurs in many situations and is a cause for concern? Well, we can't possibly know the answer on the basis of a brief observation alone. That's why we need information from you—the parent—to help us place the behaviors we observe within the context of what *you* know about your child.

You know your child better than anyone else on earth. You see him in the morning and at night, in familiar places and new places, when he's alone and when he's with others. You see him when he's sick and well, during meals and during play, at home and in the community. You probably even watch him sometimes when he's sleeping. You know his likes and dislikes, his habits and patterns, his needs and moods. And you know in your gut when something is just not right. So in this chapter, I've gathered together information that will equip you to become a careful and objective observer of the early symptoms of autism so you can help your child's health care professionals more accurately identify—or rule out—autism as early as possible.

THE EARLIER THE BETTER

Although research has revealed that autism can be diagnosed accurately as young as twenty-four months, the average age at which children receive a definitive diagnosis of autism is still three to three-and-a-half years. This has to change. I certainly understand why parents who feel "something" is wrong will turn away from that gut feeling as long as possible, hoping their child will outgrow it. It's so hard to say out loud, "My child is not developing as she should."

Unfortunately, a late diagnosis of autism robs children and their families of invaluable opportunities for improvement along many cognitive and emotional pathways, while the brain and behaviors

By the Numbers

The Centers for Disease Control and Prevention and the Metropolitan Atlanta Developmental Disabilities Surveillance Program did a study to find out how the rates of autism compared with those of other childhood disabilities. The researchers found the rate of autism for children ages three to ten years to be 3.4 per 1,000 children, which is lower than the rate for mental retardation (9.7 per 1,000 children). However, the same study found that the rates for autism were higher than the rates for cerebral palsy (2.8 per 1,000 children), hearing loss (1.1 per 1,000 children), and vision impairment (0.9 per 1,000 children).[1]

are still developing. Children with autism who participate in early intervention programs that are structured, specialized, and consistent can show dramatic improvements in their skills and behaviors. If you have a feeling that something is wrong, for your child's sake, you cannot keep that to yourself. *Early intervention is the key to optimal outcomes for young children with autism.*

What Are the Early Signs?

If you're worried that your baby under twelve months of age is not developing according to standard expectations, you most certainly should bring your concerns to the child's pediatrician without feeling like an alarmist. Sure, family and friends will assure you that all babies are unique, that you can't compare one to another, and that undoubtedly your baby will soon catch up with the others—and they may be absolutely right. But every day, scientists are learning more and more about the symptoms of autism that show themselves in infancy—and it's important for parents and health care professionals to be aware of them as well.

A recent study led by Lonnie Zwaigenbaum of McMaster University in Ontario, Canada, for example, was designed to identify behaviors of infants at twelve months that distinguished those children who later received a diagnosis of autism from those who did not.[2] The researchers compared later-born siblings of children with autism (who are at higher risk of developing autism themselves) to children from the general population (who are expected to show typical developmental patterns). The babies were observed and evaluated from six months of age through twenty-four months. Those siblings who were later diagnosed with autism did in fact—as a group—demonstrate several distinct differences from the other children by the age of twelve months. On average, they

- Showed less eye contact with others
- Had more difficulty with visual tracking (watching an object as it moved from side to side in front of their face)
- Showed less social smiling
- Had reduced social interest overall
- Were less likely to imitate actions of others
- Obtained lower scores on language measures
- Were described by their parents as showing more frequent and intense distress reactions

These findings are very interesting because they may provide some important clues to improve early detection. However, we can't really jump to conclusions based on the results of one study. First of all, it could be the case that these findings apply only to this particular sample of children in Ontario and won't be found by researchers working in other settings. We can feel more confident about conclusions when many different research groups obtain similar results, that is, when the study is replicated.

Also, it's important to realize that these differences were found when *groups* of children were compared. We can't yet use this information to say which combination of the seven behaviors listed (if any) will predict a later diagnosis of autism for an *individual* twelve-month-old child. These behaviors may end up being the earliest signs of autism—or they may not—but either way, all developmental concerns such as these should be discussed with your pediatrician and noted in the child's medical records to track his or her progress over time.

How Early?

Please understand that even though our knowledge about the earliest signs of autism is increasing, in most cases the diagnosis of autism is not made before the age of two. That's because the accuracy of an autism diagnosis has been studied systematically only in children as young as twenty-four months. Research has found that experienced clinicians can generally agree about whether or not a two-year-old child has autism (though they may not always agree about whether the specific diagnosis is Autistic Disorder or PDDNOS). We also know that an autism diagnosis made at age two is pretty stable over time, whereas we don't yet know how reliable or stable an autism diagnosis is in children under twenty-four months.

Some clinicians will say that they have diagnosed children with autism at much younger ages, say eighteen months, or maybe even fourteen months. And yes, I have personally seen children at around fourteen or fifteen months about whom I was concerned. But no one has yet studied in a systematic way whether the diagnosis is accurate or stable at these young ages. Our gold-standard diagnostic tests were not designed to be used with children this young. So right now it is really hard to tell whether those very young children about whom we have concerns will end up having autism or perhaps another type of developmental disorder (as further explained in Chapter Three). Luckily, there are lots of researchers (including myself) who are working hard to find the earliest signs of autism, so that the diagnosis can be made accurately at younger ages.

I know, however, that my optimism about the future won't help you today. And I understand that with the fear of autism looming over every child born these days, it is infuriatingly difficult to wait for that first smile, first word, first hug—and then the next and the next. Yet there's no way around it: the diagnosis of autism requires time and patience because it is based solely on observations of behavior, without any sort of blood test or biological markers to lead the way.

Remember that autism is a behavior-based diagnosis. So if you're worried about your young baby's development, you certainly should be observant and keep a written record of any behaviors that you think are unusual compared to other children. These observations will become very important as all the pieces begin to fit together as the child grows.

Why Is Early Diagnosis So Important?

Some people have asked me why we bother to diagnose autism in two-year-olds, as receiving this diagnosis can be so upsetting to parents. There are some who believe that it is not necessary to identify these children until it is time for them to start school. The answer to this question is extremely important!

Early detection is vital for getting children *ready* to start school. The younger the child is identified, the greater the impact that intervention is likely to have. Brain development is most readily influenced early in life. We want children with autism to be able to attend a regular kindergarten class with the other children their age in the neighborhood. And their best chance of doing this is for them to receive as soon as possible autism-specialized intervention that will give them the skills necessary for navigating the complex social demands of the school setting.

Autism is not a dead-end diagnosis; early intervention does improve outcomes. After facing the initial heartache of hearing the words, "Your child is showing some signs of autism," most parents come to understand that early detection is a positive thing. It actually gives them an opportunity to do something concrete that may change the path of their child's development for the better.

But early detection is not without its challenges, as explained in the next section.

RESEARCH TODAY

You might wonder: If the diagnosis of autism can't be determined definitively until age two, then how can we identify the symptoms of autism that appear before that age? It isn't easy! There are three main approaches to studying the earliest emerging symptoms, and each has advantages as well as limitations:

1. **Retrospective parent reports.** *Asking parents of children who already have a diagnosis of autism to answer questions about what their child was like before his or her second birthday.* Because parents know their children best, parent reports are an important source of information. However, it is very difficult for any parent (especially those of older children) to remember intricate details about their child's behavior once many years have passed. Also, the knowledge that their child has autism may color their memories of earlier behaviors, especially as they learn more about what children with autism are "supposed" to be like.

2. **Home movies.** *Watching early videotapes made by parents of children who already have a diagnosis of autism.* Videotapes that were made before age two, prior to the time the children received a diagnosis, are less likely to be influenced by the parents' knowledge about the characteristics of autism. However, the tapes that parents save may represent the child's "best" behaviors, rather than

RESEARCH TODAY, *continued*

the child's typical behaviors. Also, the situations in which the videos were made (for example, during play with toys, during mealtime, during a birthday party, on a vacation) can differ greatly from home to home—and can make a big difference in the type of behaviors that are observable from one tape to another.

3. **Prospective studies of "high-risk" children.** *Following young children who are identified as being at elevated risk for autism over several years.* Young children may be at high risk either because concerns are raised during a developmental screening or because they are born into a family that already has a child with autism. Studying later-born siblings of children with autism over time can be especially informative because these children can be followed from birth. It is expensive research, though. Because only about 5 percent of these siblings will have autism, large numbers of children must be studied to gather information from enough children who do receive an autism diagnosis. Also, the younger the age at which a child is enrolled in the study, the longer (and more costly) the follow-up period is until a definitive diagnosis can be made.

THE CHALLENGES OF EARLY DETECTION

It is easier to make an accurate diagnosis of autism when a child is four or five years old than it is when he or she is two. For starters, the *DSM-IV* criteria were not developed for very young children, so they must be adapted by clinicians in ways that are not yet standardized across the medical community. In addition, the following challenges must be met.

False Leads

You'll remember from the last chapter that the *DSM-IV* criteria for autism fall into three categories:

1. Social interaction and relating
2. Language and communication skills
3. Restricted and repetitive behaviors

Behaviors in the third category are often easiest to identify—but when considered on their own, tend to be least useful in identifying autism in young children. Certainly, it's easier to notice hand flapping or body rocking than it is to notice a child's lack of responsiveness to a smile. But restricted and repetitive behaviors occur in many young children *without* autism, and they are not universally observed in children who *do* have autism in this age group.

It's true that children with autism may develop an unusually intense interest in a particular item—toy cars or shoelaces, for example. But children *without* autism may also become attached to certain objects, such as a favorite blanket or a collection of rocks. My own son does not have autism, but starting at about eighteen months (and lasting about two years!) he developed an excessive interest in fans. He would enter people's homes and run into each room looking for ceiling fans, then count them and stare at them as he turned each switch on and off repeatedly. We kept him away from large hardware stores because if he spied the ceiling fan display in the lighting department, we couldn't get him out of the store. As if that weren't enough, his first word combination was "round and round," in reference to a fan he was watching at the time. This behavior certainly seemed unusual, but I wasn't worried about autism because it was one of *many* ways he liked to entertain himself; it occurred within the context of other play behaviors that were creative and flexible, and in the context of age-appropriate social and communication skills. So the presence of a repetitive behavior in isolation is *not* a sure sign of autism.

And certainly many typical two-year-olds enjoy repetitive activities and routines. At this age, all children like routine schedules, especially for bedtime and waking-up time. If a toddler's nighttime routine follows a snack–bath–pajamas–bedtime story order, pity the poor baby-sitter who doesn't know that— changing the order can just ruin the night!

Even repetitive motor activities are not uncommon for children in this age group. They may run around in circles over and over again just for the fun of it. They may twist their body in unusual positions just to see what it feels like. And they may flick their fingers in front of their eyes to see how it makes things look. When it comes to body movements, some young children are just plain quirky, but that's not a medical disorder.

So the fact that a child has some unusual behaviors is not diagnostic in and of itself. They can be false leads. The diagnostic significance of these behaviors can be understood only within the context of the rest of the child's behaviors across different settings. How much time does the child spend on fan-related activities? Does he spend most of his waking hours looking at fans or looking at books that have pictures of fans or spinning objects that look like fans or making fan-shaped objects with play materials? Or does he engage in lots of different play activities, with fans occupying his time for just a small portion of the day? Are the fan activities limited only to home, or do they occur in lots of different settings throughout the day? What happens when you try to interrupt his fan activities? Is it easy to redirect him to different toys or activities, or does he become very upset if you try? To what extent does his interest in fans disrupt your family's activities? And perhaps most important for a diagnosis of autism: What are the child's social interactions like? Does he enjoy and seek out interactions with others? Is he easy to engage in playful activities?

What is different about the repetitive behaviors of children with autism is the intensity with which the child pursues them and the fact that they occur *along with* social and communicative deficits. If a child's social and communication skills are good, it doesn't matter what "odd," "weird," or "unusual" behaviors he has as far as a diagnosis of autism is concerned.

Hidden Symptoms

The behavioral symptoms in the social and communication categories are the most reliable early indicators of autism in young children—but they can also be the most difficult ones to observe.

The social and communicative deficits seen in children with autism represent the *absence* of expected behaviors rather than the *presence* of unusual behaviors. The failure to smile back at a parent, the failure to show off for attention, the failure to imitate the actions of an older sibling are so much harder to pick up—especially in a clinical setting.

Angela, for example, looked like a typical two-year-old when I first saw her at the clinic. I was immediately taken by her beautiful blue eyes and angelic face—her name certainly fit her appearance. She sat at a small table playing with a pile of wooden blocks. While babbling away to herself the whole time, Angela picked up the first block and dropped it on the floor, then the next and the next until the entire collection lay at her feet. Was this a repetitive behavior? Or was this a typical toddler experimenting with gravity and practicing the art and joy of language? Based on this brief observation alone, there was nothing about her outward appearance or behavior that I could latch on to and say "Ah ha! This child has autism."

I needed to know more about the behaviors I didn't have an opportunity to observe by simply watching her play alone. For example, I needed to see how she interacted with her parents and how she interacted with me. What would Angela do when her parents were in the room with her? Would she continue to play with the blocks, or would she try to get her parents to play with her? What would she do if her parents tried to get her to play a different game?

And how would she respond to me? Could I get her to smile by acting goofy? Could we have fun playing together? If she was having fun, would she look at me and smile to let me know her feelings?

If I stopped a game she liked, would she let me know that she wanted me to continue? I needed to know much more about the things I couldn't see, and gaining that knowledge would take time and lots of input from Angela's parents.

Further, social symptoms are hard to identify because we don't have the same kinds of precise definitions of milestones for social behaviors that we have for motor skills or language skills. We know that children are supposed to walk by around one year and are supposed to talk by two years of age. But when are children supposed to smile responsively, show off for attention, or show empathy by patting a crying baby? We simply don't have a map to follow when it comes to social behaviors. The availability and awareness of language milestones in our culture may be one reason why delayed language development—and not delayed social development—is the most common early symptom reported by parents of children who end up receiving a diagnosis of autism.

It's Not All or Nothing

The symptoms of autism are not the kind that are either there or not there. The behaviors that are disrupted in autism are complicated. It isn't the case that children with autism *never* smile at you or look at you—sometimes they don't, but sometimes they do. The difference between the social behavior of two-year-olds with and without autism is a matter of subtle degrees.

Young children with autism can definitely show some of the same age-appropriate social and communicative behaviors that other children do—but there are qualitative differences in the way those behaviors are expressed. Sometimes the difference is the *consistency* with which children with autism show these behaviors. For example, they may imitate words just as clearly as other children—it's just that they do it less often. And they may look at their parents and laugh after the little clown in the jack-in-the-box pops out—but they may not use these same behaviors to share enjoyment with their parents during any other activities. So the behaviors look the same when they occur—but they don't occur with the same frequency or across a wide range of settings as they do for typical children.

Other times, the difference between the social and communicative behaviors seen in children with autism and in those without has more to do with the *effort* that parents have to make in order to elicit them. Take smiling at parents as an example. Young children with typical development often smile at their parents spontaneously. They may do it when their parent walks into the room or when the parent gives them something they like. They may smile to interact, to communicate pleasure, or to get a certain response from their parents. Getting a smile from the child takes very little effort on the part of parents of typically developing children.

In contrast, parents of children with autism often have to work much harder to get their child to smile at them. A child with autism may not smile until his mother makes a concerted effort to draw his attention to her, and even then may smile only during a favorite physical game or routine such as a tickle game. It's just not as easy.

And still other times, it's the *inflexibility and lack of variety* of social behaviors that differentiates children with autism from their peers. Thirty-two-month-old Cassie, for example, was a bundle of contradictions. Her parents were concerned because she showed some of the signs of autism they had read about, yet at other times she seemed like a typical two-year-old. For instance, her mom, Diane, had read that children with autism do not engage in imaginative play, yet she thought Cassie was very imaginative. She would spend hours each day arranging pencils to form letters of the alphabet. And she acted out scenes from her favorite videotapes. Yet her older sister could not get her to play with dolls, have a tea party, or play dress-up.

Diane also heard that children with autism don't know how to communicate in order to get what they want, but Cassie did. Although she didn't talk much, she knew how to communicate. She would take her mother's hand and bring her to the door when she wanted to go outside to play. She would bring her mother a toy to fix if it wasn't working. Yet she never communicated with her mother unless she wanted something. She never communicated to get her mother to look at her or play with her or show her the pretty drawing she had made.

Diane had also read that children with autism aren't affectionate, yet Cassie was just crazy about her dad. The two of them would chase each other, wrestle, and laugh all the time. Cassie would also climb up on her mom's or dad's lap when she was tired or upset and needed some loving. But when either of her parents initiated the affectionate behavior, she showed little interest. She pulled away from their hugs and would let them hold her only for short periods. This was so frustrating! Each day, Diane woke up hoping that that would be the day Cassie would be consistent in the way she acted so that Diane could know for certain whether or not her little girl had autism.

The following list of "dos and don'ts of early detection" summarizes what we've discussed in this section:

Do	Don't
Become familiar with the behavioral symptoms that are used to diagnose autism	Expect your pediatrician to make a diagnosis during a routine office visit
Be aware that the expression of symptoms can vary from child to child	Talk yourself in or out of the diagnosis on the basis of comparing your child to another
Observe your child's social and communication skills across different situations and with different people	Jump to conclusions because your young child shows some repetitive behaviors or interests
Talk to your pediatrician and request an assessment as soon as you suspect symptoms of autism	Hold off on mentioning your concerns to the pediatrician if you see a pattern of impaired social, communication, and play skills

SYMPTOMS OF AUTISM IN CHILDREN UNDER AGE THREE

In the past ten years there has been a great deal of research focused on the characteristics of autism in children under three years old, so our knowledge in this area has increased dramatically. Studies have relied on the reports of parents as well as on the direct observation of children in structured and naturalistic settings. A summary of social, communication, and play behaviors that have been found to occur less often in young children with autism than in children with typical development or developmental delays is presented in Figure 2.1.

Impaired Social Interaction and Reciprocity

All young children with autism have impaired social interaction and reciprocity skills. These impairments show up in their interactions with other children as well as with adults. But even children under age three with *typical* development don't show the same range and quality of social behavior that older children do. So let's look at what type of interactions we can expect (and would be smart not to expect) of typically developing children this young as compared to children with autism.

Social Interaction.   Typically developing children under age three show interest in their peers—they like to watch them, play near them, and sometimes interact with them for short periods. Even at young ages, children have a social "drive" that leads them to seek out and be with others and to experience these social interactions as enjoyable.

However, no children at this young age have the social understanding or insight to form true friendships. They aren't yet able to understand the concept of sharing or loyalty—both important to the bonds of friendship. And they can't yet empathize with others or take the perspective of another child (or any person, for that

FIGURE 2.1. Behaviors That Occur Less Often in Two-Year-Olds with Autism.

Social

- *Looking at others during interactions*
- Showing off to get their parents' attention
- *Smiling for social purposes (to share their enjoyment or in response to a smile or praise from others)*
- Repeating actions that lead to laughter and attention from others
- Attempting to please parents
- Showing interest in other children (watching them, playing near them, or playing with them)

Communication

- Using gestures (such as shaking their head "no," waving good-bye, or shrugging their shoulders) to communicate
- Using facial expressions (such as a surprised or disgusted look) to communicate
- *Directing attention to share their interest in something (not to request something) by pointing to or showing objects*
- *Following the direction of another person's point*
- *Responding when their name is called*
- Following simple directions

Play

- Imitating the actions of others
- Playing with a variety of toys in diverse ways
- Engaging in functional play, especially with dolls
- Engaging in imaginative play

Note: Italicized items indicate behaviors that have also been found to occur less often in children under twenty-four months (who receive a later diagnosis of autism).

matter!). They are egocentric—the world revolves around them and their own needs. It's not because they're selfish; it's because they haven't reached the stage of brain development in which intuition and altruism guide their interpersonal behavior. So when a child hits a playmate, she doesn't do it with the understanding that the other child will feel pain. Nor is she able to consider the consequences of her actions, such as having to sit in "time-out" or losing time on the playground or receiving a scolding from a parent. She does it impulsively, because she is angry or wants something the child has, or maybe even because the child hit her first.

Although all young children are egocentric and impulsive with their peers, they do, at this age, show social interest and an ability to engage with other children, even if only for brief periods. Children with autism, however, show less interest in watching or imitating other children and have less social drive. They are less likely to experience their social interactions as fun or rewarding.

This egocentric view of the world held by typically developing children under age three applies to interactions with their parents also. Young children view parents as a source of comfort, security, and protection. They don't view parents as people who have independent thoughts, desires, and needs. So when your two-year-old has a temper tantrum in a store, he doesn't do it with the intention of upsetting or embarrassing you—in fact, he doesn't have the ability to understand at all how his tantrum will make you feel. He does it because he wants a toy or wants to leave or wants to stay—or because this behavior worked the last time to get him what he wanted! Tantrum behavior is common and understandable for a child of his age.

Young children with autism also do not see their parents as separate beings with independent thoughts, but they often do not even try to engage their parents' attention. They do not try to please them or anger them or get them to do things for them. They often seem to be more focused on the objects around them than they are on their parents.

Reciprocity. The *DSM-IV* describes one of the social deficits of children with autism as a lack of social or emotional reciprocity. Reciprocity refers to a mutual or cooperative interchange between people—a two-way, back-and-forth relationship.

How does a typical two-year-old child express reciprocity? He or she does so through participation in back-and-forth games and through the interactive mirroring of behaviors and emotions. Infants engage in reciprocal interactions by laughing when their mother imitates their actions or facial expressions and by trying to imitate those of their mother. They engage in back-and-forth chatter with adults long before they learn how to talk or have a conversation. They smile when their parents (or even strangers) smile at them, and sometimes they become agitated when their mothers stop smiling or looking at them.

This reciprocity also occurs when they're a little older and they start to play simple lap games, such as peek-a-boo, and to imitate their parents' hand movements during songs like "Itsy Bitsy Spider." These are all enjoyable activities for both the child and parent, involving the exchange of positive emotions: the parent's pleasure stimulates a pleasurable feeling in the child, and the child's pleasure stimulates the same response in the parents.

For children with autism, this back-and-forth interaction and the resulting emotional connection doesn't seem to be as strong. Yes, these children may experience enjoyment and pleasure while riding on a backyard swing, but they are less likely to share this pleasure by turning to their parent and smiling to communicate their happy feelings. And yes, these children may experience a sense of accomplishment when completing a difficult puzzle, but they are less likely to bring it to their parents and show it to them with pride in their eyes. They don't show off to make their parents laugh or imitate the actions of peers to get an interaction going. In fact, many children with autism would just as soon play with objects as engage in interactions with other people.

As one parent mentioned to me, "He shows no interest in his baby sister—it's like we brought home a piece of furniture."

> ☼♡☼ **PARENTS SAY**
> **About Social Skills**
>
> - It's hard to get his attention—he likes to do his own thing.
> - He doesn't warm up to strangers easily.
> - She is happiest when left alone.
> - We just can't reach him.
> - He seems to be in his own little world.
> - Everything she does is on her own terms.
> - She knows when other kids are in the room, but ignores them.

Impaired Language and Communication

Nearly all children with autism have a delay in the development of spoken language. But even before signs of language delay become apparent, young children with autism may show delays in the communication skills that precede language—the use of nonverbal forms of communication, such as gestures, eye contact, and facial expressions. Figure 2.2 presents a list of language (and prelanguage) milestones that typically occur between birth and age three. Children with autism often do not meet these benchmarks.

Before they begin communicating through the spoken word, children with typical development figure out ways of getting what they want nonverbally. Some will point to their cup on the counter when they are thirsty; others will take a parent by the hand and walk to the toy cabinet when they want to play; others will bring the parent their shoes when they want to get dressed.

But young children with autism who do not yet have language can have great difficulty communicating their needs nonverbally. They may simply fuss or jump up and down and screech, rather than indicate in a specific way what it is they want. Sometimes it's

FIGURE 2.2. Language Development Milestones.

The stages of language development vary from child to child—with or without autism. Therefore, remember that this list is no more than a *guideline* of milestone ages.

One Month
Cries mostly to express displeasure.
Makes throaty sounds.
Looks closely at parents when they talk.

Two to Three Months
Cries now express needs, such as wet diaper, hunger, cold, and so on.
Makes cooing noises.
Will "talk" with babbling noises and chuckles.

Four to Five Months
Laughs to express pleasure.
Combines vowel and consonant sounds, like "ah-goo."

Six to Seven Months
Repeats one-syllable sounds such as "da," "ma," "mu," and "di."
"Talks" when others are talking.

Eight to Nine Months
Listens to familiar words.
Begins to combine syllables such as "dada" and "mama" but does not yet attach any meaning to them.
Understands the word "no" (but does not often obey it!).
Responds to simple verbal commands such as "give me" or "clap."

Ten to Eleven Months
Says and understands "dada" or "mama."
Says and understands "bye-bye."
Says one or two other words besides "dada" and "mama," such as "hi," "no," or "go."
Shakes head "no."

Twelve to Seventeen Months
Recognizes objects (bottle, doll) by name.
Follows simple directions accompanied by gestures.

Answers simple questions nonverbally.

Points to objects, pictures, and family members.

Begins to use intonation to express meaning such as surprise, fear, or happiness.

Tries to imitate simple words.

Says two to three words to label a person or object, though pronunciation may be unclear.

May repeat the same word over and over again.

Eighteen to Twenty-Three Months

Points to simple body parts such as "belly."

Starts to combine words such as "more cookie."

Begins to use pronouns such as "mine."

Says eight to ten words.

Two to Three Years

Says about forty words at twenty-four months.

Uses two- to three-word phrases.

Answers simple questions.

Knows pronouns such as "you," "me," "her."

Begins to use plurals such as "shoes" or "socks."

Begins to use regular past tense verbs such as "jumped."

At thirty-six months, can use up to nine hundred words and sentences that average three to four words.

---

easier for them to figure out how to get things themselves than it is to communicate their needs and desires to others. One parent told me that her two-year-old child carried around a stool, which he used to climb up on counters and shelves so he could reach things by himself, rather than try to enlist the help of others.

When they do communicate, children with autism are more likely to do it for the purpose of getting something they want rather than for the purpose of sharing their interest or experience with others. For example, they may request to watch a videotape by pulling their parent by the hand to the TV. Or they may request help operating a pop-up toy by putting their parent's hand on the knob they have trouble turning. Often these behaviors are not accompanied by a look to the adult, as they are in children with typical development. In fact, children with autism are sometimes described as using other people's hands as tools, as if they are not attached to a person.

Although they may bring toys to parents when they need help with them, young children with autism will rarely hold up a toy and show it to their parents just because they think it is cool and want to share that information with them. Similarly, even if they are able to point to out-of-reach objects to request them, young children with autism will rarely point to objects just to indicate their interest, such as by pointing to the moon in the sky or the dog across the street.

Some children with autism do develop some spoken language before age three, but they may show unusual language characteristics. They may echo what they hear others say, long after their peers have passed through this language learning stage. They may not have the language flexibility that other children have, and may use the same word to mean many things. For example, a child with autism may use the word "okay" at various times to mean "Do this" and "Help me" and "I want that."

☼♡☼ PARENTS SAY
About Language and Communication

- He gets things by himself.
- He can't tell me what he wants.
- She takes my hand and pulls me to whatever it is she wants.
- He repeats lines and songs from videos but has no concept that this is language.
- We thought she couldn't hear.
- He is always jabbering, but doesn't use words to communicate with us.

They may repeat words they've heard in other contexts, such as the child who walks to the door and says "The end" to indicate that his time in this room is over and he wants to leave. Like their prelanguage skills, the language of children with autism tends to be used to get things from others rather than to share an experience or feeling with them. Other times, they may use words nonsocially just to hear the sound of them, rather than to communicate with another person at all.

Restricted and Repetitive Behaviors

Typical two-year-olds have strong imaginations. They love to make toy planes fly, to have toy cars transport little people from one place to another, and to take care of teddy bears and baby dolls by hugging and feeding them. They have no trouble at all turning a towel into Batman's cape or pretending to cook a plastic hamburger.

Many two-year-olds with autism, however, do not use toys in functional ways (the way they were designed to be used) and do not show the variety of imaginative activities that their peers do. Instead, young children with autism may use toys in repetitive ways or may not show interest in toys at all. They may line up their little toy people in the same order over and over again, but never actually play with them as if they were people. They may open and close and open and close the doors on a toy car, or spin and spin the wheels on their truck, but never push the vehicles forward to an imagined destination. They may spend lots of time dumping toys out of their boxes and scattering them around on the floor. Or they may not show interest in any of the toys their parents have bought them, but prefer to play with household objects instead, such as the Tupperware bowls or even the doors on the kitchen cabinets.

But as my own son's interest in ceiling fans shows us, these restricted or repetitive activities alone are just not enough to warrant an autism diagnosis in children under three years old. If, however, they occur along with deficits in social skills, communicative skills, or both, they are important pieces of the whole picture.

♡ PARENTS SAY
About Restricted Activities

- He plays with all of his toys by lining them up.
- She studies things very carefully.
- She shuts out everything else when she's interested in something.
- He plays by dumping his blocks and then putting them back again—over and over.
- He likes to drop objects and watch them fall.
- He's a creature of habit—likes to have everything in its place and in order.
- He hasn't figured out toys yet, but enjoys exploring in cabinets and drawers.

A STORY OF EARLY DETECTION: PART ONE

Jeff and Judy came to our clinic with their twenty-eight-month-old son, Luke. They first became concerned about Luke's behavior when they noticed that at the age of eighteen months he wasn't talking at all the way his older sister had at that age, and that instead of wanting to play with other children in the neighborhood, he spent hours on end alone, entertaining himself in his room.

When they spoke to their pediatrician about their concerns at that time, she recommended that Luke be seen by an audiologist, to make sure that his hearing was intact. End result: it was. Their pediatrician then reassured Jeff and Judy that boys can develop language more slowly than girls, and she encouraged them to wait until Luke's next medical checkup at twenty-four months to see how his language was developing before pursuing additional evaluations.

While waiting for something to change, Judy read an article about autism and began to wonder if this could be the cause of Luke's language and social problems. He seemed to have some of the described symptoms—but not all. This is what she told us.

Right now, Luke is an enigma. There are some things about him that are so typical of a two-year-old, and other things that I just don't understand at all. I noticed that Luke doesn't try to get my attention by bringing me or showing me things like his sister did. He just ignores me most of the time unless he wants something—and then he will lead me by the hand to what he wants. For example, he pulls me over to the TV and then fusses until I find the right tape to put in. When he needs help with a pop-up toy, he will put my hand on the part he wants me to push. On rare occasions he will say "op" for "open" when he wants help, but he rarely looks at me when he makes such a request.

Luke is a playful kid, but again in what I think are unusual ways. Most often he plays by himself. He likes to watch TV, especially the commercials. (I think it may be because he likes the music.) He sometimes jumps up and down and flaps his hands while he watches. He also loves to write with a pencil or pen, but it's odd that he won't touch crayons. He definitely likes to hold thin objects (especially sticks) in each hand, and he sometimes arranges them in different ways in front of his eyes.

Luke's dad and I have a real hard time understanding why Luke doesn't want to play with us. He seems so hard to reach. His dad is sometimes able to connect with him by tickling him or playing a swinging game. Then Luke will sometimes give a real hearty laugh and look at us to share his enjoyment. That happens rarely, but when it does it means so much to us. Luke likes these games so much that he'll actually back up into us to communicate that he wants to be swung, or he'll place Jeff's hand on his tummy to request more tickles. Just lately he started playing a peek-a-boo game with me in which he moves his head behind a chair and smiles when I "find" him. He likes to play it when it's his idea, but I can't get him to play if I initiate it.

I think Luke is pretty smart. He's only two, but he can count to ten and he knows all his letters. He likes to look at books, but again he doesn't like to share that activity. He won't sit on our lap to let us read to him. I love my son so dearly; I want to hold him close and sing to him and read to him—but he just won't let me. But does that mean he has a developmental disorder or just that he's an independent child?

At his twenty-four-month checkup, Luke's language skills had not improved, so the pediatrician decided to refer Luke to specialists who would conduct a comprehensive developmental evaluation. This process is carefully explained in the next chapter, and we'll follow Luke and his family through the system. But before they arrived for their first appointment, Judy and Jeff filled out a Parent Observation Checklist that was later used to help the clinicians better understand Luke. Figure 2.3 is a copy of their form. I've also included a blank copy, Figure 2.4, for your own use as you move on to Chapter Three. The purpose of this checklist is to help you develop a rich, detailed description of your child's social-communicative behaviors. It is not a test, and there is no "score." It's a tool to help you better observe your child's behavior, and it's an objective recording of your concerns that will help your child's health care professionals determine if an evaluation for autism would be appropriate.

YOU TRY IT

In Chapter Three, you will find that your observations of your child's behavior are vital to ruling in or ruling out the diagnosis of autism. The Parent Observation Checklist printed here (Figure 2.4) is one concrete way to help you take an objective look at your child, and it will also help the health care professionals better understand your concerns. (Before you begin to check off your observations, you might want to make a few copies of the blank form. Then you will have additional ones if you'd like to repeat the process at a later time.)

FIGURE 2.3. Luke's Parent Observation Checklist.

Instructions: Observe your child for a week, across different situations and with different people. Estimate the frequency with which your child exhibits each of the behaviors listed below. Following each item, write down situations in which your child is *most likely* and *least likely* to show the behavior.

	Rarely	*Sometimes*	*Often*
1. When you smile at your child, does s/he smile back?	☐	☑	☐

Most likely times: *If I'm also tickling him; when I sing the alphabet song*

Least likely times: *If I'm just talking to him—usually he won't even be looking at me*

2. When your child is playing by him/herself and you call his/her name, does s/he look at you?	☑	☐	☐

Most likely times: *Only if I get in his face or make some kind of noise*

Least likely times: *When he's watching TV or playing with his sticks*

3. When you point to show your child something, does s/he follow your point?	☐	☑	☐

Most likely times: *If I'm close to him and actually touch or tap on it; if it's something of high interest, like bubbles or letters*

Least likely times: *If I'm pointing to something in the distance*

FIGURE 2.3. Luke's Parent Observation Checklist, *continued.*

	Rarely	*Sometimes*	*Often*
4. When you try to join in your child's play activities, does s/he share his/her toys and play interactively with you?	☐	☑	☐

Most likely times: *If it's a toy that's not one of his favorites— but only briefly*

Least likely times: *If I interrupt him while he's looking at a book or playing with his sticks*

	Rarely	*Sometimes*	*Often*
5. When you show your child a different way to play with a toy, does s/he watch you and then try it?	☐	☑	☐

Most likely times: *Only if it makes a sound or lights up or does something*

Least likely times: *If it involves imagination or play with dolls or stuffed animals*

	Rarely	*Sometimes*	*Often*
6. When a familiar adult greets your child, does s/he respond by looking at the person?	☐	☐	☑

Most likely times: *If it's Grandpa Bill, who he's very attached to*

Least likely times: *If it's someone he doesn't see often or know well*

	Rarely	*Sometimes*	*Often*
7. When your child is enjoying an activity, does s/he look at you and smile to indicate his/her pleasure?	☐	☑	☐

Most likely times: *During peek-a-boo or tickle games—but not consistently*

Least likely times: *When he's watching TV or playing one of his favorite solitary activities (looking at books, playing with sticks)*

	Rarely	Sometimes	Often

8. When you laugh at something
   your child does, will s/he repeat
   the action to see if you will
   laugh again?   ☑   ☐   ☐

   Most likely times: *I've never seen him do this*

   Least likely times: *?*

9. Does your child point to things
   or show you things just to
   share his/her interest or
   excitement with you?   ☑   ☐   ☐

   Most likely times: *The closest thing is when he brings me a toy that he*
   needs help with—but that's to get me to do some-
   thing for him, not to share anything with me

   Least likely times: *?*

10. Does your child try to get
    you to play with him/her,
    such as handing you toys
    while looking at you?   ☐   ☑   ☐

    Most likely times: *Sometimes he will hand me a book or a ball as if he*
    wants to interact, but after I take it he just walks
    away—usually he's not looking at me anyway

    Least likely times: *When he's entertaining himself with his solitary*
    activities

11. Does your child approach
    other children and try
    to play with them?   ☐   ☑   ☐

    Most likely times: *He'll go near them if they have a toy he likes or*
    if they're doing something he likes to do (like go
    down the slide at the park)—but not just to interact
    with them; he will sometimes approach his sister to
    get her to play a chase game with him

FIGURE 2.3. Luke's Parent Observation Checklist, *continued.*

	Rarely	Sometimes	Often

Least likely times: *When there is a large or noisy group of children—*
he'll keep his distance

12. Does your child look at you
when you are talking to
or playing with him/her?

| | ☐ | ☑ | ☐ |

Most likely times: *During peek-a-boo or tickle games, or sometimes*
when I sing the alphabet song

Least likely times: *When he's occupied in his own play activities—he*
will ignore me

13. Does your child play with
toys or other objects in
unusual ways?

| | ☐ | ☐ | ☑ |

Most likely times: *When he plays his games with sticks*

Least likely times: *?*

14. Does your child move his/her
hands or body in unusual ways?

| | ☑ | ☐ | ☐ |

Most likely times: *When he's excited he flaps his hands and jumps up*
and down; he used to spin around but doesn't do
that anymore

Least likely times: *?*

Note: This checklist is *not* designed to be a formal screening for autism and has not been validated for use in that manner.

FIGURE 2.4. Parent Observation Checklist.

Instructions: Observe your child for a week, across different situations and with different people. Estimate the frequency with which your child exhibits each of the behaviors listed below. Following each item, write down situations in which your child is *most likely* and *least likely* to show the behavior.

	Rarely	*Sometimes*	*Often*
1. When you smile at your child, does s/he smile back?	☐	☐	☐
Most likely times:			
Least likely times:			
2. When your child is playing by him/herself and you call his/her name, does s/he look at you?	☐	☐	☐
Most likely times:			
Least likely times:			
3. When you point to show your child something, does s/he follow your point?	☐	☐	☐
Most likely times:			
Least likely times:			
4. When you try to join in your child's play activities, does s/he share his/her toys and play interactively with you?	☐	☐	☐
Most likely times:			
Least likely times:			

FIGURE 2.4. Parent Observation Checklist, *continued*.

	Rarely	Sometimes	Often
5. When you show your child a different way to play with a toy, does s/he watch you and then try it?	☐	☐	☐

Most likely times:

Least likely times:

| 6. When a familiar adult greets your child, does s/he respond by looking at the person? | ☐ | ☐ | ☐ |

Most likely times:

Least likely times:

| 7. When your child is enjoying an activity, does s/he look at you and smile to indicate his/her pleasure? | ☐ | ☐ | ☐ |

Most likely times:

Least likely times:

| 8. When you laugh at something your child does, will s/he repeat the action to see if you will laugh again? | ☐ | ☐ | ☐ |

Most likely times:

Least likely times:

| 9. Does your child point to things or show you things just to share his/her interest or excitement with you? | ☐ | ☐ | ☐ |

Most likely times:

Least likely times:

	Rarely	Sometimes	Often
10. Does your child try to get you to play with him/her, such as handing you toys while looking at you?	☐	☐	☐

Most likely times:

Least likely times:

11. Does your child approach other children and try to play with them?	☐	☐	☐

Most likely times:

Least likely times:

12. Does your child look at you when you are talking to or playing with him/her?	☐	☐	☐

Most likely times:

Least likely times:

13. Does your child play with toys or other objects in unusual ways?	☐	☐	☐

Most likely times:

Least likely times:

14. Does your child move his/her hands or body in unusual ways?	☐	☐	☐

Most likely times:

Least likely times:

Note: This checklist is *not* designed to be a formal screening for autism and has not been validated for use in that manner.

FREQUENTLY ASKED QUESTIONS

Why do more boys than girls receive a diagnosis of autism?

We know that boys are at least four times more likely than girls to have autism, but we don't yet know exactly why. Boys are also more likely than girls to show the milder behavioral features that are referred to as the broader autism phenotype. In fact, autism is not the only disorder that shows this gender bias—dyslexia and Attention-Deficit/Hyperactivity Disorder also occur more commonly in boys than girls. We know that male and female brains develop differently and that some of these differences can probably be attributed to genes on the X chromosome (females have two X chromosomes, and males have one X and one Y chromosome) and genes related to sex hormones.

Many genetic studies have been conducted to try to understand the reason for the sex differences in autism, and it has become clear from this research that no *simple* genetic mechanism can account for this phenomenon. One interesting theory put forth by Dr. Simon Baron-Cohen, of Cambridge University, is that prenatal levels of the male hormone, testosterone, may determine whether an individual has a predominantly "male brain" or "female brain." The male brain is characterized by a tendency to "systematize" (identify how things work), whereas the female brain is characterized by a tendency to "empathize" (identify and relate to the feelings of others). Individuals with autism are described as having an "extreme male brain" because of their unusually strong drive to systematize and weak drive to empathize. Baron-Cohen believes that exposure to too much testosterone before birth may contribute to the development of autism; he has called for additional research to test this theory.

My child was diagnosed with autism at age two, and now that he's four, I'm told that all he has is a language disorder, not autism. Was he misdiagnosed at age two?

The amazing thing about early intervention is that it really seems to work! Early interventions that are autism-specialized can lead to symptom improvement in lots of areas, including those on which the diagnosis is based. Intervention approaches that involve teaching the child new skills and teaching the parents how to help their child during everyday routines can be very effective in improving children's social interactions, communication, and behavior.

It is possible that at age two your child had a language disorder and not autism. His language disorder, in combination with his temperament, may have led to social and behavioral difficulties that resulted in a diagnosis of autism. With intervention and over time, he may have learned to communicate more effectively as well as to regulate his emotions and behavior better, to the extent that his behaviors no longer met the criteria established for autism.

It is just as likely, however, that his behaviors at age two were in fact diagnosed accurately as autism, and that the intervention he received was successful in changing his path of development. Perhaps he received just the right type of social and communication intervention at just the right time to take advantage of the flexibility and "plasticity" of his still-young brain. We know that experiences can influence brain development, so it is certainly possible that he no longer meets diagnostic criteria for autism because of the intervention he received.

Because we have no way to see into or predict the future, I feel that it's best to err on the side of caution, which means providing autism-specialized services for children who show characteristics of autism at age two.

Do children with autism suffer from seizures?

About one in four children with autism may develop seizures during childhood or adolescence. Seizures, which are caused by abnormal electrical activity in the brain, can produce a temporary loss of consciousness (a "blackout"), body convulsions, unusual movements, or staring spells. Seizures are not particularly common in children with autism who are under age three—rather, the onset of seizures is more common in later childhood or in adolescence. However, if your child seems to have staring spells that are difficult to interrupt, it is critical that you discuss this with your pediatrician immediately, to see whether further evaluation is warranted.

Is extreme sensitivity to sounds or touch a sign of autism?

Although it is not mentioned specifically in the *DSM-IV* as a symptom of autism, some children with the disorder are described by their parents as exhibiting unusual behaviors related to one or more of their senses. Sometimes children appear to be hypersensitive to sensory stimuli, and other times they seem to be underresponsive. Some children with autism do not like to be picked up or held and are very sensitive to the way that clothes feel on their body. At the same time, they may crave the sensation of deep pressure. One parent described her child as putting "his hands into the bends of our knees and elbows, or under the couch cushions, to feel pressure on them." Some children with autism seem to be unaware of pain and do not react even when seriously injured.

Children with autism can react in unusual ways to auditory stimuli as well. Some can't tolerate the sound of thunder, fire engines, or the vacuum cleaner, and others seem almost deaf to the sounds around them. By themselves, these sensory differences are not a sure sign of autism, but if they occur along with impairments in social and communication skills, then the unusual sensory features are something the child's health care providers will add to their observations to help determine the final diagnosis.

TAKING THE NEXT STEP

There is good news in the autism arena. Even if your Parent Observation Checklist indicates a reason for concern, remember that autism is not a yes-or-no, black-or-white disorder, and it certainly is not a dead-end diagnosis—especially when detected early. So if you have concerns about your child's development after reading this chapter and using the Parent Observation Checklist, it's time to take the difficult, but important, step toward a medical evaluation.

In the next chapter, you'll see what you and various health care professionals can do to determine or rule out autism.

3

THE EARLY DIAGNOSTIC PROCESS

For many parents, there comes a day when they can't ignore the gut feeling that their child is not like others. If you're one of these parents, you know you've tried so hard to get your child to laugh, play peek-a-boo, and wave bye-bye. You've encouraged her to say "cookie" and "dada." But you get so little back. Still, like many of the parents I've met at the clinic, you might be afraid to open the door that will answer the question "Why?" You might fear that once you do that, there's no turning back. I certainly understand why you might feel that once you say aloud, "I'm concerned my child may have autism," life will never be the same for you or your family.

That's how Dave felt for so many months before he was finally willing to talk about his daughter's behaviors with her pediatrician. "I kept hoping that Katie would wake up one day and everything would be fine," remembers Dave. "It was obvious early in infancy that she was somehow different from my brother's child of the same age, but it was just so hard to admit my worries out loud. I guess I thought that if I didn't say it, maybe it wouldn't be so."

Dave is quick to admit that if his wife hadn't been so insistent about her concerns, Katie would not have gotten an early diagnosis of autism and, thankfully, early intervention. Says Katie's mom, Sue,

Dave and I would sometimes argue about Katie's behavior. He just kept making up excuses for all the things that I was worried about, and—I admit—I often wanted to believe he was right. Maybe Katie was just shy. Maybe she was exceptionally smart, and that's why she focused on things so intently. Maybe Katie was just one of those kids who didn't talk right on time. Maybe. Maybe. Maybe. But when Katie still wasn't talking at the twenty-four-month checkup and when I really looked at how many of her behaviors didn't seem developmentally right, I just wasn't willing to wait and see any longer. I didn't want to upset my husband, but I also wasn't going to ignore the pediatrician's recommendation to get Katie a comprehensive developmental evaluation. As much as I didn't want to take this next step, I also didn't want to let my own fears get in the way of what my daughter needed.

If you believe that your child has developmental delays but are worried about taking this next step, I certainly understand. But I encourage you to do it. I hope that after reading through this chapter you'll feel more comfortable about what to expect from the diagnostic process and confident that you have the information you need to move forward and get your child the evaluation he or she needs.

APPROACHING YOUR CHILD'S DOCTOR

If your child is showing some of the symptoms discussed in Chapter Two, then the first step in the diagnostic process is to talk to your child's primary care doctor about your concerns. This person is usually a pediatrician or family practitioner, but for the purpose of this book, I will refer to him or her as a pediatrician. As your child's primary health care provider, the pediatrician will coordinate your child's health care needs. This coordination role includes evaluating your concerns, ruling out medical causes for problems, making referrals for evaluations, and advocating for the most appropriate services for your child.

If your child is very young, say under age three, you may have to be the one to first bring up the subject of autism to your child's pediatrician in order to take advantage of the benefits of early detection and intervention. Sometimes pediatricians can be as hesitant as parents to open the door to the evaluation process. When delays in speech first become obvious, some pediatricians may encourage parents to be patient and give their children time to catch up, which may be good and appropriate advice—but also may not. Moreover, because the word *autism* is so emotionally loaded, pediatricians can be very hesitant to bring it up to parents as a possibility. They certainly don't want to upset a family and then find out later that the child is simply on his or her own developmental curve or has a case of shyness or a treatable hearing impairment.

Keep this in mind if your child's pediatrician does not mention the "A word" even when you ask questions about your child's delayed development. This silence has caused many a parent to go home after a well-baby checkup and report to his or her spouse, "I told the doctor about the baby's delayed speech and odd behavior, and he didn't mention anything about autism, so I guess that's not something we should worry about."

If after reading Chapters One and Two you have serious concerns about your child's development and the pediatrician doesn't seem particularly concerned, don't take a passive approach. *You* must be brave and be the one to say the word "autism" out loud. Once *you* say the word, the subject can then be objectively discussed, and you and the pediatrician together can decide what next step to take.

So take a deep breath and read on. In the following sections you'll learn what to expect after you say, "I'm worried that my child has autism."

Using the Parent Observation Checklist

The Parent Observation Checklist (Figure 2.4 in Chapter Two) can be a good way to introduce your concerns to your child's doctor if he or she has not been the first to mention the possibility of autism.

Given the brief period of time allotted for checkup appointments, your pediatrician may not be able to read through the form and analyze your answers on the spot. But you can use it to describe your observations and concerns and read through a few examples you've noted.

Most pediatricians will not diagnose a developmental disorder (unless they have a specialization in developmental pediatrics), but should recognize the symptoms and refer a child for further evaluation with the appropriate specialists. Many professional organizations, including the American Academy of Pediatrics, have advocated early identification of autism and provide guidelines for when referrals should be made for further evaluation. The American Academy of Neurology, for example, lists the following red flags as requiring immediate referral.[1]

Red Flags for Immediate Evaluation

- No babbling by twelve months
- No gesturing by twelve months
- No single words by sixteen months
- No spontaneous two-word phrases by twenty-four months
- Loss of language or social skills at any age

The Proactive Physician

If you have indicated a number of concerns on the Parent Observation Checklist, your pediatrician may take action immediately, understanding that early detection is vital for improving your child's outcome. Exactly how the pediatrician will proceed will certainly vary from one physician to the next, but what follows is an overview of some typical steps you can expect as you begin the evaluation process.

Step One: Use Screening Tools. One approach your pediatrician may take is to use a screening tool to evaluate the behaviors of concern. Scores on screening tools help the doctor determine the best course of action.

Several screening tools have been developed to identify children who are at risk for developmental disorders. These measures do not provide a diagnosis, but are designed so that a "positive" screening result suggests the need for further evaluation. The advantage of screening tools is that they provide a more objective, standardized way of evaluating concerns, compared to a pediatrician's subjective impressions during a brief office visit. Screening tools are developed by comparing the behavioral reports or observations of children who have certain developmental disorders to those who do not; thus it's possible to determine whether a child's score is more similar to the scores of children with or without the disorder.

There are several types of screening tools. Some are general, broad-spectrum tools, designed to screen for developmental delays across a wide range of areas (such as language, motor, and problem-solving skills). Others are autism specific and focus on identifying children who are at risk for autism in particular. Some are based on parental reports, others on observations of or interactions with the child (see Table 3.1).

In the context of an office visit, most pediatricians will choose to use parent-report screening measures because they can be completed and scored more quickly. One of these screening tools is called the Modified Checklist for Autism in Toddlers, or M-CHAT.[2] The M-CHAT was developed for and tested on children twenty-four months of age. It consists of twenty-three yes-or-no questions for parents to answer. The pattern of responses determines whether or not the child is at risk for autism. A copy of the M-CHAT, along with scoring instructions, is provided in Appendix B. If you decide to fill out the M-CHAT, I have two very important suggestions for you: (1) don't peek at the scoring system before you complete the questions, so your responses will be more objective; and (2) don't panic if your child's score falls in the "at risk" category. Here's why:

TABLE 3.1. Examples of Screening Measures for Young Children with Suspected Developmental Disorders.

	Parent-Report Measures	*Interactive Measures*
Broad spectrum	Parents' Evaluation of Developmental Status (PEDS)	Battelle Developmental Inventory (BDI)
	Ages & Stages Questionnaire (ASQ)	Developmental Assessment of Young Children (DAYC)
Autism specific	Checklist for Autism in Toddlers (CHAT)[a]	Checklist for Autism in Toddlers (CHAT)[a]
	Modified Checklist for Autism in Toddlers (M-CHAT)	Screening Tool for Autism in Two-Year-Olds (STAT)
	Pervasive Developmental Disorders Screening Test-II (PDDST-II)	

[a]The CHAT is based on both parent report and clinician observations.

Screening tools are designed to cast a wide net, to identify all children who *may* be at risk for a disorder. That means that the tool will identify some children as at risk when they don't really have the disorder (called false positives). At this early stage in the identification process, it's better to overidentify some children as at risk than to miss children who actually have the disorder (false negatives). So we can expect that some children who are identified as at risk for autism on the M-CHAT will turn out not to have autism during their follow-up evaluation. They may receive no diagnosis at all on follow-up or may receive a different diagnosis, such as language delay. Because screening tools are not infallible, it is also possible that some children (usually those with milder symptoms) will be identified as not at risk when they actually do have autism. So if your child's score indicates no risk but you remain concerned, it's still a good idea to pursue a full evaluation.

You may be wondering how the Parent Observation Checklist and the M-CHAT are different. The purpose of the Parent Observation Checklist is to guide your observations of your child and to provide you with important information about your child's social and communication development that you can discuss with your pediatrician and other clinicians during the evaluation process. It is descriptive. There are no right or wrong answers, no scores to indicate your child's risk status. The Parent Observation Checklist helps you describe the behaviors you are concerned about and the situations in which they occur. In contrast, the M-CHAT provides a score that indicates whether the child is at risk or not at risk for autism. So these two tools provide very different, but complementary, types of information for parents who are concerned about their children.

Step Two: Obtain Medical Evaluations. In response to parental concerns, positive screening results, or both, the pediatrician will next explore medical reasons for the developmental delays or concerns. For example, he or she may assess the possibility of lead poisoning (which can cause developmental delays), especially if the child is known to eat nonfood items and has spent time in older buildings that may contain lead-based paint. In addition, the child may be referred to an audiologist to rule out a hearing problem. Although you may be anxious to move ahead more rapidly and get right to an autism evaluation, at this early stage the pediatrician is making sure there are no other possible causes for your child's developmental delay—and that's an important precaution. (See Table 3.2 for examples of evaluations that may be recommended by your pediatrician.)

Because language delays are often one of the earliest concerns, it is likely that your pediatrician will also refer your child for a speech-language evaluation. If the evaluation reveals a delay or disorder in

TABLE 3.2. Examples of Professional Evaluations
That May Be Recommended.

Professional	Type of Evaluation	Purpose of Evaluation
Audiologist	Hearing evaluation	To rule out hearing impairment as a cause of language delays
Speech-language pathologist	Speech-language-communication evaluation	To rule out physical defects in the mouth and other oral structures as a cause of language delays
		To identify the presence, type, and extent of speech, language, and communication impairment
Psychologist	Cognitive and developmental evaluation	To assess the child's level of cognitive functioning
		To identify the child's strengths and weaknesses in different areas
	Diagnostic evaluation	To determine whether the child's behaviors are consistent with a *DSM* diagnosis
Geneticist	Genetic and metabolic testing (blood test)	To rule out genetic disorders (such as fragile X syndrome) or metabolic disorders (such as PKU) as causes of developmental delays and behavioral symptoms
Neurologist	Neurological evaluation; includes physical exam and may include such tests as EEG or MRI if indicated	To rule out the presence of a progressive neurological disorder (if regression is present)
		To rule out the presence of a seizure disorder

language understanding or use, the speech-language pathologist may recommend that your child receive speech therapy. That's not a bad idea, but some parents then go off with this recommendation as their only course of action. It may not be enough. If your child has language delays along with social or behavioral impairments, he or she should also be referred for an autism evaluation.

In some cases, pediatricians may refer children for a genetic or neurological evaluation. A child may be referred for a genetic evaluation if

1. There is a family history of developmental disorders (such as mental retardation) or genetic disorders associated with autism (such as fragile X syndrome).

2. The child demonstrates a pattern of behavioral regression that may indicate a metabolic disorder (such as inborn errors in amino acid metabolism).

3. The child has physical features that are unusual in shape or size (dysmorphic)) or exhibits medical or behavioral symptoms that might be consistent with a known genetic disorder.

Your pediatrician may recommend a neurological evaluation if your child demonstrates evidence of (1) behavioral regression or loss of skills, (2) behaviors suggesting the possibility of seizure activity, (3) disordered sleep patterns that may have an underlying medical cause, or a combination of these.

Step Three: Refer to State Early Intervention Program. Instead of referring children directly for speech-language or diagnostic evaluations, some pediatricians may take an alternative approach to the referral process. After the medical evaluation, your pediatrician may refer you directly to your local early intervention (EI) service program for assistance obtaining evaluations and any needed services. These programs are funded by each state as one of the provisions in U.S. Public Law 105-17, the Individuals with Disabilities Education Act. Although different states have different names for these programs and the organization and implementation of these services differ from state to state, this law requires that every state have a network for identifying young children with disabilities and for coordinating their services. Under this act, EI services are to be made available to infants and toddlers with disabilities from birth through thirty-five months of age.

This state system of care can be extremely helpful to parents because it offers service coordination, provides referrals for evaluations and intervention, and covers some of the costs involved. Through this program, your family will be assigned a service coordinator, who will ensure that your child receives the evaluations and interventions that he or she needs, at least until the age of three. As your child approaches three years old, the service coordinator will refer you to other agencies (often the public school system) for help as needed.

The Watch-and-Wait Physician

There are some physicians who still prefer the watch-and-wait approach, hoping to give children more time to develop their skills. Before the promising results of early intervention were understood, this was standard protocol. In fact, one study found that of thirteen hundred families surveyed in 1997, the average age at diagnosis of autism was about six years, despite the fact that most parents felt something was wrong by the time the child was eighteen months of age, and usually asked for a medical opinion about their concerns by age two.[3]

Fortunately, early detection is much more common now, but still not all pediatricians are eager to refer children before three or four years of age. In that case, *you* can be proactive and tell your child's doctor that you want to move forward now with an evaluation by a specialist.

Be insistent. This is your child. You have to be proactive to get him or her the proper diagnosis as soon as possible—and also to take advantage of the services available through the state EI program. If you've come this far in the book, you know there's a sense of urgency to get a definitive answer, and sitting back to "watch" for the next year or two is not that answer.

When parents insist, most physicians will give the necessary referral. But if your child's doctor remains reluctant, you're still not at a dead end. Of course it is best to work as a team with your child's medical professionals, but if that's not happening, you can move on without them. You can contact your local EI program yourself. Your pediatrician's office will have the phone number, and a physician's referral is not necessary for this step in the process.

GETTING THE MOST OUT OF DIAGNOSTIC EVALUATIONS

Diagnostic evaluations can take place in different settings and can be conducted by different types and combinations of clinicians. The most common evaluation settings are private-practice offices, community-based clinics, or diagnostic clinics affiliated with universities or medical centers. Regardless of the setting, the goal of this referral is the same: to rule out other developmental disorders whose symptoms are often confused with those of autism and to carefully identify those pointing specifically to autism.

The diagnosis should be made by a professional who has been trained in the use of the *DSM-IV*; in most cases this is a child psychologist, child psychiatrist, or developmental pediatrician. Sometimes the diagnosis is made by a single clinician, and sometimes it is made in the context of a multidisciplinary team. Multidisciplinary teams are usually found in clinics based at medical centers; they might include a psychologist, developmental pediatrician, speech-language pathologist, social worker, occupational therapist, and physical therapist.

Although it is appealing and often advantageous to have all the different evaluations take place during one visit, it is becoming

♡ PARENTS SAY
About Asking for an Evaluation

- We began testing for hearing loss and communication delays at eighteen months old. The "A word" came up once early on, and I fell apart. After that, it was a series of denial, seeking people who told me he was NOT autistic, and staying away from moms of autistic children who were telling me to have him tested. It finally hit me when a therapist said to me, "So what if he is autistic? What will that word change about him? He is who he is, and has the needs he has. You already know all of that. Besides, with the diagnosis, you will be allowed so many more opportunities for help than you have without it." After that, we never looked back; we have pressed into this thing with a vengeance, and he is blooming. (parent of three-year-old boy)

- It took about six months between the time that I first suspected autism and the time we received my son's diagnosis. My feelings at the time were varied: I experienced impatience, sadness, acceptance, and above all a curiosity about autism that created a strong desire for more knowledge. (mother of twenty-six-month-old boy)

- I had not realized how far behind my child really was until those tests were presented to me. I wish I had known ahead of time that autism is treatable and that the symptoms vary greatly with each individual. (father of four-year-old boy diagnosed at three-and-a-half) increasingly difficult to obtain multidisciplinary evaluations due to limitations in the reimbursement rates of the health care system. Multidisciplinary clinics are very expensive to operate, and reimbursement from insurance companies is usually not adequate to cover expenses. Therefore, you may have to go from one specialist to another, which is a more time-consuming and piecemeal approach.

Because autism is a very complex disorder and is difficult to diagnose in young children, it is critical that you find professionals who have experience with autism and its manifestations in young children. Your pediatrician or service coordinator may make a recommendation to a specific clinician, but you should still do some homework before you make an appointment.

If you have health insurance, you may be expected to have your child evaluated by a clinician whose name appears on a list supplied by your health insurance company. Although it may be important to find a doctor who participates in your health care plan, this is not the time to choose a name randomly from the insurance company Web site. With the list of participating clinicians in hand, take the next step to identify those with the expertise you need.

The personal referral of a friend or preschool teacher is always good to have. But if that's not available, you can begin your search for qualified professionals through the Autism and PDD Support Network (www.autism-pdd.net) or the Autism Society of America (www.autism-society.org). Both of these sites have "Resources" links that lead to a state-by-state listing of professionals, state agencies, and other resources. This kind of search can help you narrow down your choices.

The Autism Society of America also has local chapters. By contacting parents in the chapter in your area, you may be able to learn more about local clinicians and services. Talking to other parents who have been in your situation can be very helpful when you are just beginning the process of evaluation and diagnosis. Of course, if you contact other parents, keep in mind that one parent may have had a very positive experience with the same clinician that another parent disliked. But a personal recommendation gives you at least a good place to start.

Finding a clinician who has experience working with young children with autism is not always easy—especially if you live in a rural area. In that case, it may be worth your time to focus your search on the nearest major city that has a large medical center; there you'll be more likely to find clinicians specializing in autism. Unfortunately, some children do not get the help they need because their parents trust local clinicians who, though well intentioned and certainly adept in their field, are just not up on the latest in autism diagnosis and care. At our diagnostic clinic in Nashville, Tennessee, we see many families from other parts of the state, as well as those from surrounding states. These parents know that connecting with clinicians who are trained and experienced in working with young children with autism can have a major impact on the quality of their child's future.

When you begin to contact clinicians to make that first appointment, ask this important question: "I'm looking for someone who is comfortable making a diagnosis of autism in young children and who has training and experience in this area. Can you tell me about your qualifications in this area?" The responses you get will help you choose the most appropriate clinician to evaluate your child.

The following is a summary of the steps you can take to ensure that your child is evaluated by professionals who routinely work with children and who have experience with children with autism:

- If you have medical insurance, get your company's list of participating clinicians.

- Get recommendations for clinicians who *specialize* in children with autism from your pediatrician, other parents, your child's teacher, or your local chapter of the Autism Society of America.

- Contact potential clinicians and ask about their comfort level and expertise with the diagnosis of autism in young children.

WHAT TO EXPECT

When you find an experienced professional and make your first appointment, you're a giant step closer to getting an answer to that difficult question, "Does my child have autism?"

To get the most out of that first visit, gather all the information you've compiled so far in the process, including any screening forms you have completed and any evaluation reports you have received. Examples include the Parent Observation Checklist, the M-CHAT, audiological and speech-language evaluations, and any other developmental screenings that have been conducted. Sometimes clinicians or diagnostic evaluation centers will ask you for this information in advance. These previous evaluations will help clinicians not only determine the most appropriate tests to give but also interpret their results in light of previous findings.

The exact procedures used during the diagnostic evaluation will vary from one clinician and setting to another, but there are some similarities that can help you know what to expect.

- First of all, you can expect the evaluation to take several hours. There's no rushing it. There will be several components to the evaluation, and your child will be given lots of breaks, as needed. It may be helpful to bring your child's favorite toys, snacks, or comfort items with you to the evaluation. When you make the appointment, it's a good idea to ask how long these evaluations usually take, so that you can be prepared.
- Second, you can expect that the child will not do everything during the evaluation that he or she does at home. This is natural, and experienced clinicians know it. That's why they will ask *you* so many questions about the child's typical behaviors in everyday situations. This inconsistency in your child's performance occurs for several reasons. One is that the clinic is an unfamiliar

setting, and young children don't always show their stuff in less familiar environments. Another reason is that standardized tests require that instructions or questions be presented in a specific way, which may be different from the way you usually say or do things at home. For example, the child may be accustomed to the instructions "*Show me* the dog," but the clinician may say "*Point to* the dog" instead. Or your child may be asked to name colors using pictures in a book, instead of labeling the colors of puzzle pieces that you use at home.

• Third, you and your child may be seen by several different professionals during the course of the evaluation (especially if it takes place in a medical center), which may feel a bit overwhelming. In teaching settings, such as medical centers, trainees may conduct some or all of the assessments. (These trainees may be medical students or residents, clinical psychology graduate students or interns, or child psychiatry fellows.) Don't worry if this is the case; the trainees will be observed and supervised by licensed professionals and will interpret the results in collaboration with their supervisors. In these settings there may also be other observers during the evaluation, such as trainees who are not yet ready to administer the evaluations themselves.

• Fourth, you may not receive the results of the evaluation on the same day. Different clinics have different procedures. You should ask about this when you make the appointment so that you are not disappointed if you have to wait before receiving your child's evaluation results. Ideally, you should not have to wait more than a week for the clinician to give you the results verbally; however, the written report may take longer.

• Fifth, it is important to know that several sources of information will be used to make the diagnostic determination. In addition to reviewing previous evaluations from other caregivers or service providers, the clinicians will also use information from parents, from standardized testing, and from the clinician's careful behavioral observations of the child. Each of these components of the evaluation is described in this chapter.

PARENTS SAY
About Getting a Diagnosis of Autism

- My concern for my son's development came in waves. We were stressed about it his first six months or so, and so his doctor ran lots of physical tests (for digestive disorders, hearing problems, etc.). Then, he seemed to get a little better when he began crawling. So we tried to relax about it. Then we got concerned again a little after his first birthday, wondering if it was him or us that had the problem. We got his diagnosis of autism at about age two, so there wasn't a lot of time between that first "definite red flag" and diagnosis (about six months). I actually felt somewhat empowered during this period because I was finally starting to feel that I wasn't inadequate or crazy but rather that there was something going on and, most importantly, I could do something about it. When we finally got the diagnosis, I was relieved. I know lots of parents panic and go into denial when they hear "autism," but I latched onto the idea because it was something real and legitimate, not just my imagination. I could say to myself, "I'm not just impatient and intolerant and selfish; my son has autism." (mother of five-year-old boy diagnosed at two years)

- What was most helpful in the diagnostic process was being able to watch and participate. As questions were asked, I was finally able to breathe and realize I wasn't crazy! The questions were pointing out areas I knew were a bit quirky, but couldn't

THE PARENT INTERVIEW

The parent interview usually begins with a description of your concerns. What caused you to seek a diagnostic evaluation? Why now? Which behaviors seemed consistent or inconsistent with what you have read about autism?

This is your opportunity to explain your concerns in detail. Because autism cannot be diagnosed through any objective medical test, your input regarding your child's behaviors and development is critical to the process. This is another time that the Parent Observation Checklist can be very helpful for describing your child's behaviors and expressing your concerns. The clinician will probe for behaviors in the areas of social and communication development and for repetitive, restricted activities. He or she may use a structured interview, such as the Parent Interview for Autism[4] or the Autism Diagnostic Interview-Revised[5] to gather this diagnostically relevant information.

During the interview you will also be asked about your child's medical history. There will be questions about whether there were any birth complications, whether your child has had any major illnesses or hospitalizations, whether he or she has any allergies or is currently taking any medications. You will be asked when your child first sat up, walked, and said his first word. You will be asked about behaviors related to your child's eating, sleeping, and toileting habits. Sometimes clinicians will use a standardized measure, such as the Vineland Adaptive Behavior Scales,[6] to gather information about your child's level of independence and skills during everyday activities at home and in the community. Other questions will focus on your family's history of medical, developmental, or psychiatric disorders. If you have records of this information, you should review them or bring them along. It's hard for any of us to remember all the details and dates when under the mental stress of this first visit.

COGNITIVE TESTING

A cognitive or developmental assessment is usually part of the diagnostic process. The purpose of this type of assessment is to determine your child's level of cognitive or intellectual development. Results of cognitive testing are important for several reasons. First, they provide information about a child's relative strengths and weaknesses, which can be used to identify areas of need for intervention. Second, they provide information that can be used diagnostically to help rule out other disorders that have features in common with autism.

Two of the most commonly used cognitive assessments for children under three years old are the Bayley Scales of Infant Development-II[7] and the Mullen Scales of Early Learning.[8] On these tests, a child's performance is compared to that of a large normative sample of children the same age. His or her performance relative to peers is converted into a standard score. Standard scores often have different names from test to test, and the range of scores considered

RESEARCH TODAY

Autism has been associated with increased head size in young children. A study by Eric Courchesne at the University of California, San Diego, has suggested that the rate of head growth in the first two years of life may reflect a pattern of brain development that is unique to autism and that may represent an early marker for the disorder. Specifically, children with autism were more likely than typical children to show an unusually rapid growth in head circumference between birth and the ages of six to fourteen months.[9] Because head circumference is related to brain size, this finding may point to early differences in brain development that may be causing the symptoms of autism.

A longitudinal study of head growth in children with autism is now being conducted by the Baby Siblings Research Consortium to determine whether these results will be replicated in a different sample. The consortium and this project are cosponsored by the National Institute of Child Health and Human Development (NICHD) and the National Alliance for Autism Research (NAAR).

"average" can also differ across tests. For example, for the Bayley-II and the *composite* score on the Mullen, standard scores between 85 and 115 are within the broad average range. However, for the individual *subtests* on the Mullen, standard scores between 40 and 60 are within the average range. Scores below these ranges are below average and above these ranges are above average. Age-equivalent scores can also be derived from these assessments; an age-equivalent score indicates the approximate age level at which a child is functioning. Age-equivalent scores are also referred to as "mental age" scores.

Cognitive assessments are often subdivided into different skill areas. The Bayley-II yields two separate scores, one for mental development and one for physical development. The Mullen yields five different subtest scores, in areas assessing gross motor skills (large muscle movement and coordination, such as walking and hopping), fine motor skills (small muscle movement and coordination, such as picking up small items or placing pegs into pegboards), nonverbal problem solving (such as matching, sorting, and puzzle activities), language understanding (such as following simple commands, pointing to named objects), and language expression (such as using words and gestures to communicate). It is important to note that because different cognitive assessments use different items to assess similar developmental domains, it is not uncommon for children to obtain different scores on different assessments.

I usually tell parents of young children with autism not to place too much emphasis on the specific cognitive scores their child receives. These scores give us a general idea of where the child is functioning at this particular time on this particular test. But cognitive scores of children under three years old are not necessarily stable over time, especially for young children with autism.

Still, cognitive assessments provide information that is critical for helping us distinguish between children with autism and children with other developmental disorders. Because social and communication behaviors are key to an autism diagnosis, it is important to determine whether delays in these areas can be accounted for by the child's overall level of cognitive development. If a child's level of social-communicative development is consistent with his or her development in other cognitive areas, then a diagnosis of global developmental delay may be more appropriate than a diagnosis of autism. In contrast, if the child's social and communication skills are delayed with respect to his or her overall level of cognitive development, then autism might be a more appropriate diagnosis.

A child's pattern of performance across different cognitive areas can also provide important diagnostic information. For example, young children with global developmental delays (but not autism) often obtain cognitive scores that are fairly evenly delayed in all areas. In contrast, young children with autism often show more extreme variability across different cognitive areas, with a relative strength in nonverbal areas compared to verbal or language areas. Children with autism can have global developmental delays as well, but even then their nonverbal skills tend to be stronger than their language skills.

It is very helpful for parents to observe the cognitive evaluation if possible. Some settings have one-way mirrors that enable parents to watch and listen from an adjacent room. If this setup is not available, ask if you can sit in the room with your child during the evaluation. (If your child has difficulty separating from you, the clinician will probably invite you to accompany him or her to the room anyway.) By observing, you can provide valuable input to the clinician about how typical your child's behavior was, describe any behaviors that surprised you, and tell him or her about the skills that the child usually demonstrates at home. You can also give suggestions for behavior management strategies that have worked for you at home, or simply provide a lap for your child to sit on to increase his or her comfort level.

However, there are also things that you *shouldn't* do when sitting in the testing room with the child. It is very important that you not prompt your child's performance in any way, such as by rephrasing the examiner's instructions. It is very tempting to do this, I know, but standard scores are valid only if the test is given in the proper manner, which usually means giving instructions in a prescribed way. So fight the urge!

It is also hard to resist asking the clinician how your child is doing, but you are unlikely to get the information you want in the middle of the evaluation. The clinician needs time to put together all the different pieces of information before making a diagnostic determination, so giving you information prematurely could be misleading.

As you observe, you may wonder why the evaluation seems to be taking forever or why the clinician seems to be presenting so many difficult items that the child cannot possibly do. There's a reason for this: most cognitive tests are designed so that children must fail a certain number of items before each subtest can be discontin-ued. So in instances when the child has unevenly developed skills and demonstrates a pattern such as failing two items, passing an item, failing three items, passing an item, it can take a long time to complete the evaluation!

OBSERVING YOUR CHILD'S BEHAVIOR

In addition to scoring your child's performance on specific activi-ties, the clinician will also be observing your child's behavior closely. Whereas standardized tests provide information about what your child does or doesn't do, behavioral observations during test-ing are critical to determining *how* the child approaches tasks. Is he interested in the testing materials, or would he rather play with other objects in the room? Is he able to persist to completion on dif-ficult tasks, or is he easily frustrated? How does he express his frus-tration on difficult items? What will motivate him to attempt challenging tasks: Praise? Food treats? Getting to play with a favorite toy? Is he able to follow directions or demonstrations? Is he able to use trial-and-error strategies to figure things out? All of this information is important for understanding the child as well as for generating teaching strategies. Table 3.3 shows examples of impor-tant behaviors that can be observed during diagnostic evaluations.

Of course clinicians will also be looking for behaviors that will help confirm or refute a diagnosis of autism—such as how the child interacts, communicates, uses language, and plays with toys. The clinicians will observe the child during structured activities (such as cognitive testing) as well as during unstructured activities (such as free play). The clinicians will observe the child's mood and behav-ior during their own interactions with the child as well as during parent-child interactions.

Sometimes clinicians will use standardized measures or check-lists to structure their interactions or guide their observations. For instance, the Autism Diagnostic Observation Schedule (ADOS)[10] is one diagnostic measure that is considered to be a gold standard

TABLE 3.3. Behaviors to Observe During Diagnostic Evaluations.

Area	Observations
Social interest and interactions	• Does the child show interest in or awareness of the examiner? • Does the child initiate interactions with the examiner? For what reasons? • How does the child respond to the examiner's social bids or praise? • What is the best way to get the child's attention?
Emotional expression and regulation	• What is the child's overall mood during the evaluation? • Are the child's moods appropriate to the situation? • What does the child do when happy? When upset? • Can you tell what the child's mood is by looking at his or her face? Does he or she show a variety of facial expressions? • How does the child handle transitions between activities?
Language and communication	• What is the child's level of language development? • Does the child use and understand gestures such as pointing? • For what reasons does the child communicate? • Does the child use nonverbal behaviors, such as facial expressions and eye contact, to communicate? • How does the child communicate to request desired objects or activities? • Does the child try to direct the examiner's attention to objects or events of interest?

Work strategies and habits	• Does the child remain seated at the work table for brief periods? • Does the child attend to tasks without becoming overly distractible? • Does the child attempt difficult tasks? • What is the best way to motivate the child to work? • Does the child persist on tasks to completion, or give up quickly?
Use of materials	• Does the child use materials appropriately? • Does the child imitate the examiner's demonstrations of actions with materials? • Does the child resist parting with preferred materials?
Use of senses and body	• Does the child show any unusual responses to visual, auditory, or tactile stimuli? • Does the child show any unusual or repetitive body movements?

for autism assessment. During the ADOS, the clinician uses a set of standard situations to elicit and observe the child's social and communication behaviors. A standard scoring system is then used to come up with a diagnostic classification. This measure was originally developed to provide a consistent way to provide research diagnoses, but it is also excellent for use in clinical situations.

The Childhood Autism Rating Scale (CARS)[11] is a behavioral rating scale that can also be used to guide a clinician's observations. The CARS yields a score that can fall in the range of "not autism," "mild-to-moderate autism," or "severe autism." The CARS classification should not be used in place of sound clinical judgment; there have been many times when my clinical impressions have not been consistent with the score obtained on the CARS. However, it can be a helpful addition to a comprehensive diagnostic evaluation.

Of course, even with all these carefully constructed standardized measures, the clinical setting is not an ideal location for making behavioral observations and judgments. Your child is in an unfamiliar setting. She may feel your own tension and react to that in a negative way. Or she may not show the behaviors you have just insisted were so common in her day-to-day activities. With everyone watching, both you and your child may feel pressured to "perform" in some undefined way. Knowing this in advance, you can prepare to stay as calm and relaxed as possible. An experienced clinician knows that he or she may not obtain a true or complete picture of your child during the diagnostic evaluation and will not make snap judgments. Choose your clinician carefully, for there is no substitute for the trained eyes of a skilled and experienced clinician.

To give the clinician a better picture of the child at play or in daily interactions, some parents bring homemade videotapes to the evaluation (or send them in advance). Tapes can be very helpful if they are kept short (no more than five minutes) and are recorded to show specific behaviors that are relevant to the diagnostic question. Tape the behaviors you are concerned about, such as your child's unusual play habits, or his response when a sibling tries to initiate play, or his reaction to your efforts to get him to wave bye-bye or smile. Show samples of your child at home or in the park or in a roomful of cousins. This information can help the clinician see the broader picture that is so hard to gain in the clinical setting.

THE INTERPRETIVE CONFERENCE

All this testing takes time. Of course this can be frustrating and even aggravating as you wait and wait for results, only to find that there's yet another test to take. But this in-depth evaluation process is important for two reasons: (1) autism is very challenging to diagnose in young children, and no one wants to make a mistake; (2)

in-depth testing helps determine the best intervention strategies based on the child's profile of strengths and weaknesses.

Eventually the testing will be over, and you will have your interpretive conference, during which the clinician(s) will explain the assessment results to you. In some settings you will have this conference on the same day as the evaluation. In other settings it is standard procedure to ask parents to return for the results at a later time. If it is a team evaluation, this is also the time that the team members share their results and impressions with each other to formulate the diagnosis and recommendations. It is very frustrating to wait. I know. And even if you receive the results on the same day, there will be some wait time after the testing activities have been completed. Clinicians need this time for scoring the tests and for putting all the information together to come up with the answer to your question, "Does my child have autism?"

Whether you get the results that same day or have to come back another day, this can be the hardest time of all for you. No matter how prepared you are to accept the final diagnosis of autism, it is still painful to hear the word.

In some cases, a single clinician will sit down with you to discuss the results of the evaluation. In the case of team evaluations, there may be several clinicians in the room. (If the number of people makes you uncomfortable, let them know so they can make other arrangements for conducting the interpretive conference.) The conclusions that are presented to you during the interpretive conference should represent an integration of information from the test results, the clinical observations, and the information you provided. The child's strengths as well as weaknesses should be described. Results should be interpreted within the context of how typical the child's behavior was during the evaluation. The clinician should give you lots of examples of how your child's behavior was or was not consistent with a diagnosis of autism.

During the course of the interpretive conference, the clinician should check with you to see if what he or she is saying makes sense to you and is consistent with your impressions of your child. Even if the clinician doesn't ask, you should feel free to provide comments and ask questions. The interpretive conference should take the form of a two-way, interactive discussion between you and the clinician. Ask as many questions as you need to. Some parents bring a list of questions with them and go through them one by one. *You need to understand what the clinician is saying because you will probably soon be in the position of explaining it to family members, friends, and teachers.*

It is hard to predict exactly how you will react during a highly stressful situation like the interpretive conference. You may be numb and feel nothing. You may start crying and not be able to stop. You may be angry at the clinician for making what you think is a mistake—or at your spouse for dragging you to the appointment. Any reaction is okay. It's okay to be upset. It's okay to ask for a few minutes to pull yourself together. An experienced clinician will understand.

During the interpretive conference, you may also be asked if you would like the written report to be sent to anyone else. This may be hard to decide because you haven't yet seen it. It is customary for the report to be sent to the professional who referred your child for the evaluation (such as the child's pediatrician, EI service coordinator, or speech-language pathologist), but this decision is entirely up to you. The assessment information and report are confidential and cannot be released to others without your permission. In most cases, it is helpful to share the report with any service providers who are involved with your child. But if you feel more comfortable seeing the report first, you can request that it be sent just to you, then you can make copies to give to the other professionals involved in your child's care.

Whether the final answer is a yes or a no, remember that whatever you hear will reflect the state of your child's development at that moment. Although the diagnosis of autism is relatively stable over time, some children will show behavioral improvements to the extent that an autism diagnosis no longer fits. Because young children still have a lot of growing to do, we all have to be aware that changes can still occur in this "final" diagnosis.

With that said, the diagnosis you receive at this moment in time will point you in the right direction for getting your child the most appropriate interventions to meet his or her present needs.

DIAGNOSIS: NOT AUTISM

If you are confident in the clinicians' level of experience and expertise, and they say your child does not have autism, you can then exhale. But with your next breath, you'll remember that the developmental issues that started you on this quest are no doubt still present in your child. Your child may therefore get a diagnosis of another developmental disorder, such as a language disorder or global developmental delay.

If that's the case, follow-up therapies to meet the specific needs of that developmental problem will be suggested and should certainly be acted on. I would suggest, however, that you continue to monitor your child's social and communication development. If you continue to have concerns about autism, you can seek a second opinion or ask for a reevaluation in six months or a year.

DIAGNOSIS: PDDNOS

In young children it can be very difficult to differentiate between the diagnostic categories of Autistic Disorder and Pervasive Development Disorder Not Otherwise Specified (PDDNOS). The symptoms of these two disorders are very much alike and often overlap.

So it's possible that you may be told, at this point, that your child has PDDNOS. If that happens, the information about early intervention and at-home training in the following chapters still applies. Intervention strategies for children with PDDNOS and Autistic Disorder are similar, if not identical, especially at young ages.

DIAGNOSIS: AUTISTIC DISORDER

Even when parents expect to hear a diagnosis of autism and try to prepare themselves for it, receiving the formal diagnosis can still come as quite a blow. You may even go through a lengthy grieving process that is similar to the stages associated with the death of a loved one: shock, denial, anger, guilt, and depression.

The clinician delivering this news should be well aware of the shock you will experience. Even proactive parents who do their homework and recognize the symptoms themselves still feel pain when that last shred of hope is officially severed. Because it's difficult for parents to take in anything after the diagnosis is received, some clinicians will give them time to adjust emotionally before mapping out the next step. They may set a follow-up appointment to talk about the details and implications of the child's diagnosis, for the present and the future. During that time, you may also be referred to the Autism Society of America for further support and information. The local ASA chapter may have meetings, support groups, and additional information and resources. (See Resources for contact information.)

With time, you may feel a sense of relief at the diagnosis of autism. You've finally been given a reason for your child's unusual behaviors, and it can be comforting to realize that your child was not rejecting you personally but was responding to the world in the only way he or she was capable. You can get busy and do something to help your child. Now you are in the final stages of the grieving process: acceptance and hope.

TELLING FAMILY MEMBERS THE NEWS

The decision about when and how to tell family members about your child's diagnosis of autism is a very personal one. With your own emotions dangling over the edge, it's certainly difficult to say the word "autism" out loud to those who are also very close to your child. But silence isn't the solution. Others who spend time with your child need to know about his or her special needs in order to be understanding and supportive. As you talk about your child's diagnosis, always keep in mind these words I recently overheard one parent say to another: "Your child is the same child he was before the diagnosis—all the diagnosis does is help you understand and treat his behaviors." That's the message you need to convey to other children in your family and to your own parents.

Talking to Your Other Children About the Diagnosis

There is no one correct way to talk to your other children about the diagnosis of autism for one of their siblings. (Let's call the child with autism "Howie" for this discussion.) What you say and when you say it will depend on their age, whether or not they have asked questions about Howie's behavior, and the extent to which Howie's behavior interferes with family activities and routines.

A discussion about autism is something like talking to children about the birds and the bees—their readiness to hear things and their ability to understand what you tell them will change over time. As a result, your discussions are likely to be ongoing, rather than a one-time Big Talk. But at all times, it's important for you to be open to having these discussions and to listening in a nonjudgmental manner to the feelings and frustrations that your children may express.

For younger school-age children, it may be helpful to use general descriptive terms rather than the actual diagnostic label. For example, you may explain that "Howie has difficulty understanding and using words," or "Howie learns differently from the way you do," or "Howie needs help learning how to play." In the same way, without explaining all the science involved in understanding the cause of this disorder, you can assure your other children that they cannot "catch" Howie's problem behaviors.

It's also a great idea to include your other children in your at-home teaching activities (explained in Chapter Five). Show them how to interact and play with him; let them demonstrate appropriate behaviors. These "teaching" activities should be developed so they are fun for your children, rather than a chore, and it's important that you give them lots of praise and positive attention for helping.

There are also some good books about autism written for young children. These books can be an excellent resource to help you identify what information is age-appropriate for your children—and to give you the words you need to explain this very complex disorder in a simple, nonthreatening way. My advice for choosing a book is to browse through the selection in your local bookstore and find one that uses words and concepts you are comfortable with and that you would be willing to read out loud and discuss with your children.

As children approach adolescence, they will need more specific information about what autism is, what causes it, and what it means. They may be interested in reading about it and may choose to do reports about it for school. Having a child with autism in the house also gives you an excellent opportunity for discussion about understanding individual differences in all people, appreciating diversity, and talking about the positive aspects of having a child with autism as a valuable member of the family.

At the same time, your teen may be embarrassed by Howie's behaviors and reluctant to invite friends over to the house. This seemingly negative reaction is normal and should not be judged harshly—it's just a part of that difficult period called adolescence. Give your teen room to vent his or her feelings and then explain that you—more than anyone else—understand the frustration and pain. At the same time, insist that your teen treat Howie with kindness and respect.

Talking to Your Parents About the Diagnosis of Autism

Sometimes telling your parents about your child's diagnosis can be an extremely difficult task—especially with your own emotions running so high. It's hard to know what to expect; I've seen that parental reactions to this news can vary dramatically. One young mother told me, "My mother-in-law told us that we shouldn't bring my son to family gatherings until he grows up. It's heartbreaking to hear her say that she would rather not see any of us for years instead of trying to understand her own grandson." But then I've also been told, "We were very touched by how our family reacted to my son's diagnosis. Everyone asked what they could do to help, and they showed us so much support. I know his grandparents read books and articles on the disorder so they could better understand him. My mother even quit her job to help me through this very difficult time." Yes, reactions vary widely. But whatever reaction you get, it will be very important to educate your parents about the nature of autism after you have told them about the diagnosis.

To begin your discussion, you might talk about specific behaviors. For example:

> You know those behaviors we've been confused about for so long? Well, now we have a name for them and an explanation for why they occur. Howie doesn't act the way he does because he's spoiled or because he's shy or because he doesn't like us—he acts that way because he has autism. Autism explains why he doesn't speak or use gestures and why he doesn't seem to understand what we say. It explains why he's not as interested in interacting with us as the other children in the family have been, and why he plays with spoons and bottles instead of toys. I know this is upsetting news—for all of us. But the good news is that the disorder has been diagnosed early, and there are a lot of things we can do to help him. He'll be starting some therapies soon, and I'll be learning about things I can do to help him at home. I know you might need some time to take in all of this. But if you have any questions as we begin his therapy, I'll be glad to try my best to answer them. I know we're all hoping for the best outcome possible.

After the initial conversation about this diagnosis, continue to keep your other children and your parents in the information loop. Autism doesn't affect only one child—it affects the entire family.

A STORY OF EARLY DETECTION: PART TWO

We began the story of Luke and his family in Chapter Two. Luke's father, Jeff, continues it here:

> My stomach dropped when the pediatrician suggested to my wife and me that we seek a diagnostic evaluation for Luke. Does that mean that she thinks my son really has autism? Or is she just giving in to Judy's persistent questioning? A million thoughts raced through my mind. Will I never get to coach Luke on a Little League team? Will he never be able to have a job, or marry, or have children? Will he have to go to a special school? Will he end up sitting in a corner and rocking?
>
> Judy called the Child Development Center to make an appointment for a diagnostic evaluation and was told that the next available appointment was five months away. How could we wait that long? Luckily the intake person at the center referred us to the state early identification program. We met with Stacie, a service coordinator, who referred us for what felt like evaluation after evaluation.
>
> First, we had a speech-language evaluation. Luke was twenty-six months old at the time. The speech-language pathologist told us that Luke had a receptive and expressive language disorder (which means difficulty understanding what we say to him as well as using words to express himself) and that his language skills were at the nine- to twelve-month level. To tell you the truth, I don't know how she got *any* scores from that assessment—all he did was cry and run around the room. We asked about autism, but she told us that she wasn't qualified to make that diagnosis. I was a little disappointed by that evaluation because we already knew his language was behind. The good part was that we found out that he could get speech therapy right away, so at least we could start getting Luke something other than evaluations!

Our next evaluation was for occupational therapy, which I had never heard of before. The therapist worked with Luke for a while and then told us that he needed occupational therapy to improve his fine motor skills and his sensory integration (whatever that is!). I figured that more therapy wouldn't hurt, but by then we'd had a total of three evaluations in two months and we still didn't know whether or not he had autism. In the meantime, his behavior really seemed to be improving—his eye contact was better, and he was more tolerant of our affection, so maybe we were spending all this time worrying unnecessarily.

Finally the time came for our diagnostic evaluation. I tried to talk Judy out of going, but she insisted. We met with a developmental pediatrician and a psychologist and spent about three hours there. They asked us lots of questions and did a great job of working with Luke (I'd never seen him sit in one place for that long!) and then gave us the results. They told us that he had a developmental delay, that his visual-motor skills were stronger than his language skills, and that "HE HAS AUTISM." I felt like I had been punched in the stomach. I don't remember anything else we discussed that day.

FREQUENTLY ASKED QUESTIONS

I've read that some children with autism have "stereotyped" behaviors. What does that mean?

"Stereotyped" behaviors are those that are repetitive, occur often, and seem to serve no apparent purpose. They can involve body movements (such as hand flapping or body spinning), objects (such as lining up toys or spinning wheels), or verbalizations (such as repeating certain phrases from TV or videotapes). Stereotyped behaviors fall under the "restricted and repetitive behaviors" category in the *DSM-IV* criteria for autism.

How can I find information about intervention studies or clinical trials that my child may be eligible to participate in?

Several governmental agencies and private foundations post information on their Web sites about recruitment for clinical trials:

• The National Institute of Child Health and Human Development (NICHD) funds clinical trials on autism through the Network on the Neurobiology and Genetics of Autism: Collaborative Programs of Excellence in Autism (CPEA). Contact information:

Phone: (800) 370-2943

E-mail: NICHDInformationResourceCenter@mail.nih.gov
   (use AUTISM in the subject line)

Web site: www.nichd.nih.gov/autism

• For information about CPEA studies, visit any of the following Web sites:

www.nichd.nih.gov/autism/cpea.cfm

www.nichd.nih.gov/autism/research.cfm

www.clinicaltrials.gov

www.nimh.nih.gov/studies

• National Alliance for Autism Research: www.naar.org
• Cure Autism Now (CAN): www.cureautismnow.org

My friend sent me an article about a possible connection between autism and immune system abnormalities. Is there a link?

There are lots of theories about possible causes for autism (as discussed in Chapter One), but none has been proven yet. Theories are important because they generate ideas that can then be tested empirically by different researchers in different labs. But until they are proven true, they are little more than educated guesses.

One theory about autism is that it is caused by a disorder of the immune system. The purpose of the immune system is to identify and remove foreign substances (antigens) from the body. Immune system abnormalities can involve (1) a reduction in certain types of immune cells, which could limit the body's ability to fight off infection or (2) an increase in the body's autoimmune responses, in which the immune cells mistakenly identify the body's own cells as foreign and start to attack them (diabetes and lupus are examples).

Some studies have found evidence of immune system dysfunction in children with autism, but others have not, so the results are inconclusive at this point. It's important to realize, however, that even if an association between an immune disorder and autism is found, that doesn't mean that the immune disorder *caused* the autism. For example, if left-handedness and autism were found to be associated, we wouldn't be able to conclude that being a lefty caused autism. Alternative explanations for this association would be that having autism causes left-handedness or that some other underlying event caused both left-handedness and autism. (It could even be the case that autism and left-handedness have different causes that are totally independent from each other.) There are many physical conditions that have some association with autism, but be skeptical of any claim that purports to know the cause of autism—the state of science in this area just isn't there yet.

❧

Years ago, parents were told that their children with autism would end up in institutions. That is just not the case anymore. Although we don't know exactly how the symptoms of autism will progress or lessen in a child under age three, we are hoping that with early intervention, many children will be able to enroll in a mainstream kindergarten class. That's our goal. In the next chapter, you'll see the various kinds of interventions available for young children diagnosed with autism and how they may be able to help your child.

4

EARLY INTERVENTION IS YOUR CHILD'S BEST HOPE FOR THE FUTURE

There is no debate or doubt: early intervention is your child's best hope for the future. Early attention to improving the core behavioral symptoms of autism will give your child—and the rest of the family—several important benefits that you will not gain if you take the wait-and-see approach until your child enters school at age four or five. A good early intervention program has at least four benefits:

1. It will provide your child with instruction that will build on his or her strengths to teach new skills, improve behaviors, and remediate areas of weakness.

2. It will provide you with information that will help you better understand your child's behavior and needs.

3. It will offer resources, support, and training that will enable you to work and play with your child more effectively.

4. It will improve the outcome for your child.

For these reasons, an intervention program for your child should be implemented as soon as possible after he or she receives a diagnosis. However, as you probably know by now, it can be very challenging to teach young children with autism. They have a unique profile of strengths and needs and require intervention services and teaching approaches that are sensitive to these needs. That's why strategies that worked fine for teaching your other children to remain seated at the dinner table, to play appropriately with a toy, or to say words simply don't work as well for your child with autism. In the same way, intervention programs that are generic—rather than autism-specialized—are less likely to be effective for your child. That's why as you begin your exploration of early intervention, you must keep in mind that not all interventions are equal.

This chapter will help you evaluate a variety of programs to better determine which teaching approaches are best for your child.

♥ PARENTS SAY
Advice from Personal Experience

The advice I would give other parents of children with autism is this: (1) Seek therapy and dive into it like your child's life depends on it (because it does). (2) Step away from your world occasionally and breathe some fresh air. (3) Remember, your child's behavior doesn't reflect on you as a parent. The opinions of the people in the grocery store don't matter; you don't owe the world an apology when your child makes loud animal noises in the frozen foods aisle. You don't have to explain the autism spectrum to everyone who gives you a dirty look when your child licks your arm and yells, "No dancing!" to no one in particular. Is your child safe and happy? Is your child getting his needs met and being gently guided toward progress? That makes you more than a good parent—you're the parent of a special-needs child. That's what it's about. (mother of three-year-old boy)

UNDERSTANDING YOUR CHILD'S LEARNING STYLE

Finding the right intervention program begins with an understanding of your child's learning style—which is quite different from the learning style of other children. You probably realize this if you've tried to get your child with autism to wave bye-bye using the same teaching strategies you used with your other children—that is, demonstrating the action, providing a verbal prompt by saying "wave bye-bye," and even moving his or her hand to demonstrate what to do. But when that approach didn't seem to be working, you probably started to think that your child was being stubborn or uncooperative. After all, you're teaching these simple skills using methods that worked very well for your other children. But the reality is that your child isn't being bad; he or she just has a different learning style from your other children.

This difference in learning styles isn't apparent only when you try to teach children with autism; it's also evident in the way they learn (or don't learn) on their own. There are lots of things that children *without* autism seem to learn effortlessly, *without being taught*, but that children with autism don't pick up on as easily. For example, young children without autism somehow learn, without explicit teaching, how to use a pointing gesture to let you know what they want or to indicate where they want *you* to look. They learn to follow *your* point or eye gaze to figure out what you're looking at or what you're interested in. They figure out on their own how to use eye contact and facial expressions to convey their feelings—as well as to understand the meaning of *your* facial expressions and tone of voice. Social-communicative behaviors and skills like these just don't come as naturally to young children with autism and often need to be taught explicitly.

Exceptional Early Learning

Right now you might be thinking about all the things that your child with autism learned at a much younger age than other children you know. And yes, you are right: there are also things that children with autism learn on their own much faster than their nonautistic peers or siblings. For example:

- They can be very good at learning to pick out their favorite video from a stack, even when it's not in its case.
- They may learn at a very young age how to operate the remote controls to the TV and VCR so they can rewind their videos to their favorite parts (or fast forward through the parts they don't like).
- They can be very creative in figuring out ways to climb up on the counter to reach a cabinet that has their favorite cereal, or even how to use the key to unlock the deadbolt on the back door so they can go outside to play on the swing.

Clearly, these are not behaviors that you would even think about trying to teach a two-year-old child. And yet some children with autism somehow manage to acquire these skills on their own.

How can we understand this inconsistency between the things children with autism do and don't learn? How can a child who can't put different shapes into a shape sorter learn to turn on the TV and VCR, put a tape in, and push the play button? How can a child who can't understand a simple direction like "Get your coat" figure out how to unlock a door to get outside? What accounts for this unique learning style?

In a word: motivation. We all pay attention better to the things that interest us, so we become much more proficient at learning them.

Less Social Motivation

Children with autism seem to be motivated by different things than their nonautistic peers. For example, they are often more highly motivated to pursue favorite activities, such as swinging or watching a tape, than they are to interact socially. So while their peers without autism are busy trying to get their sister to play or showing off for their parents, children with autism are busy trying to reach their favorite food or play with their favorite objects. Remember, social impairments are one of the core features of autism.

I don't mean to imply that young children with autism have no interest in other people. Certainly, they have the same needs for comfort and security that other children do—and parents play a major role in meeting these needs. Your child may enjoy sitting in your lap in a certain special position, follow you around the house to be in the same room as you, or cling to you for dear life in new or unfamiliar situations. Young children with autism need and love their parents, just like other children do. But they are less driven to engage in the two-way, back-and-forth interactions that include trying to understand you or please you or share their interests with you.

And this is one of the things that makes teaching children with autism so challenging. Most young children experience the attention and approval of adults as rewarding—whether it comes from their parents, grandparents, or teachers. They're motivated to engage in behaviors that will earn the attention and approval of others. Children learn at an early age that they can please parents by doing what is requested of them. At the same time, they learn which behaviors will result in disapproval or withdrawal of attention, and eventually limit these behaviors to avoid these negative consequences. Because of their natural social interest, "time out" from attention is often a good strategy for reducing undesired behaviors in children with typical development.

But children with autism are often not as motivated to please adults. They are less likely to attend to their parents' demonstrations of how to play with a toy in a new way, for example, to obtain the parental attention or approval that other children crave. And that's why "time out" from attention doesn't work particularly well for reducing undesired behaviors in children with autism—being ignored is not a negative consequence for children who have limited social interest to begin with.

So we can't rely on social rewards alone to motivate children with autism to learn new behaviors or skills—we have to figure out other ways to motivate them. Other types of rewards we can use, for example, are letting the child play with a special toy or giving him or her a favorite snack. I will talk more in Chapter Five about how to identify motivating rewards and use them to teach your child new skills.

Less Language Comprehension

In addition to social impairments, the other behavioral characteristics of autism also affect the way these children learn. Consider the way we teach children how we want them to act. Our most natural teaching strategy is to give children verbal instructions or requests. We say "Hold up your arms" when we are trying to put on their shirts, and we tell them to put their tissue into the trash instead of throwing it on the floor. We verbally instruct them not to take toys away from other children, and we explain the reasons why. We tell them that they will get to play outside later, but not now—or that they will have to take their bath before dinner instead of after dinner. In other words, we use language to give instructions, to provide information, and to describe the behaviors we expect from them. This strategy works pretty well for children who understand language.

But what about for children with autism who have delays in language comprehension? We can't always know if they understand us, so we have to find other ways to convey these types of information. That requires different kinds of teaching methods. One such method is to provide visual supports (such as pictures) in addition to verbal requests. This strategy capitalizes on an area of strength for many children with autism—recognizing and remembering the meaning of pictures. Many children with autism are good at processing visual information, and their skills in this area can surpass those of children with typical development. Providing them with pictures or other types of visual supports gives them extra information to facilitate their understanding. In this way, we're building on one of their strengths to improve an area of weakness. The next chapter will provide additional information about how to create and use visual supports.

More Restricted Play Patterns

A child's restricted activities or interests can also influence his or her learning. Some children with autism show an excessive interest in one or two toys or objects that they play with exclusively and have difficulty parting with. Others may have a single preferred way of interacting with toys and may be very resistant to learning new ways to play with them. For example, a child may prefer to spin saucers on the table rather than place cups on them for a pretend tea party. Another may have a specific way of completing a shape puzzle and may become distressed when an adult changes the order of putting in the pieces or tries to have him label each shape before putting it in.

Some children with autism may avoid interacting with certain toys that have sensory qualities that are unpleasant to them. For example, some children with autism do not like the feel of Play-Doh or are bothered by the sound of mechanical toys. Because children are so often taught through play-based lessons, we need to make sure that we have a good understanding of each child's play patterns, preferences, and dislikes before we can develop an appropriate early intervention program for him or her.

Through the discussions later in this chapter of various types of early intervention programs, you'll see how different educational therapies are adapted to meet the unique learning needs of children with autism, with the goal of enabling them to enroll in a regular kindergarten class when they turn five. The following is a list of skills and behaviors that are expected of children in kindergarten; this will give you an idea of the kinds of skills an early intervention program strives to build.

Kindergarten Readiness Skills: Expected Classroom Behaviors

- Listen to directions from across the room
- Follow group instructions
- Comply with adult requests

- Locate materials and put them away
- Share materials and take turns
- Work and play without disturbing others
- Sit quietly in small and large groups
- Work independently and attend to tasks
- Complete assignments
- Raise hand to get attention
- Communicate needs and ask for help
- Answer questions
- Line up and walk in line
- Wait appropriately
- Make transitions between activities
- Manage self-care activities independently (eating, toileting, and so on)

Many of these skills may seem far out of reach for your child right now, but don't be discouraged. Even two-year-olds with typical development have a long way to go before they are kindergarten-ready. Parents of all two-year-olds have three years to help their children acquire the skills they need to be socially and behaviorally ready to attend kindergarten. And with early intervention, your child has time and you on his or her side. That can make all the difference.

OBTAINING EARLY INTERVENTION SERVICES

Most parents of children under three years old take advantage of the free services offered through their state early intervention (EI) program. Although the process to obtain these services can differ from state to state (or even between different regions of the same state), I thought it would be helpful to provide a brief overview here so that you have a general idea of what to expect.

State EI services typically consist of a network of different programs, each serving a designated geographical region. In many cases, parents have contacted their state EI program prior to their child's diagnosis, and their service coordinators have helped them obtain their diagnostic evaluation. In other cases, parents have decided to wait for their child's diagnosis before contacting their EI program.

Either way, the diagnosis of autism is your child's ticket to specialized services, and your EI service coordinator will work with you to help your child obtain the services he or she needs. The service coordinator will be the point person for gathering the information about your child and your family that is needed to determine your child's eligibility for services and to develop an Individualized Family Service Plan (IFSP). The IFSP is a document that serves as a road map for your family's participation in the EI system. It specifies the services that are needed, who will provide them, where they will be provided, and how often they will be provided. The IFSP also includes a transition plan that describes the services your child will receive when he or she turns three and transitions from the EI system to other programs and services offered through your local school district.

When your child enters the school system, he or she will have an Individualized Educational Plan (IEP) team rather than an IFSP team. The following are some tips for easing your child's transition from the EI system to the school system; you might want to refer back to them as the time approaches.

Prior to the actual transition,

1. Request a face-to-face meeting between members of your current IFSP team (including you!) and members of your future IEP team. It is important that people who have worked with your child have the opportunity to share information about him with the teachers and therapists who will work with him in the future.

2. Bring materials to this meeting that will help the IEP team understand your child's individual strengths and needs. For example, if your child uses visual supports, bring an example to show the team. Let the team know what types of materials or supports your child will be bringing to his new classroom.

3. Find out as much about your child's new school as you can. Visit the school and classroom (while the class is in session). Meet your child's future teacher. Learn about the routines in the new school and classroom so you can prepare your child. For example, ask questions about the class schedule, the bathroom routine, and how fire drills are handled. Find out where the children eat lunch, and what the expectations are for naptime.

4. Bring your child to the school for brief visits to see his future classroom and meet his future teacher. Discuss the possibility of having your child attend school for half days instead of full days for a short while if you think that will help ease the transition.

At this time, your child will continue to need your support and guidance. And you will need to continue your efforts as the primary advocate for your child.

Developing the Individualized Family Service Plan

Developing an IFSP is a collaborative team process. The IFSP team typically includes the service coordinator, community service providers, and parents (who may invite other family members or advocates to the meeting). The IFSP team may also include the professionals who evaluated the child and those who provide intervention services.

The content of the IFSP is based on information that includes an understanding of the abilities and needs of the child as well as the resources, concerns, and priorities of the family. The philosophy underlying EI services is that parents are critical to the development of young children. Thus the overall objectives of the IFSP road map are not only to facilitate the child's development but also to enhance the family's capacity to support the child's development.

The IFSP will contain a number of outcomes (goals) for both the child and the family, and each outcome will be accompanied by a set of action steps for achieving it. There is a heavy emphasis on providing intervention that is family centered and that occurs in the child's natural environment. (Natural environments are settings in which everyday activities and routines occur for young children and their families. They will differ from family to family and may include such locations as the home, the supermarket, the baby-sitter's house, and the park.)

The IFSP is a living document that should be reviewed at periodic intervals so that outcomes can be added or removed in response to the child's progress and changing needs. Some sample IFSP outcomes and action steps are presented in Table 4.1, but remember that the specific format of IFSPs varies from state to state, so your child's goals may look quite different.

Your input during the IFSP process is critical; this document will determine the nature of the services that your child receives. Therefore, you should prepare for this meeting in advance by thinking about what your child needs to learn in order to function well within the family and within the community. Think about which daily routines are difficult for you and your child—for example, how do things go during mealtimes, when it's time to get your child dressed, when it's time to get her to sleep? What kind of information or training do you (or other family members) need to work or play productively with your child? You need to get focused on your child and your family and arm yourself with an understanding of what all of you need.

There are a number of specific educational practices that have been associated with effective treatment programs for young children with autism. A list of these practices (compiled from several

TABLE 4.1. Sample IFSP Outcomes and Action Steps.

Outcome	Action Steps
Johanna will indicate her wants and needs to her family.	1. Speech therapist will consult with Johanna's parents about specific requesting behaviors to teach and specific prompting strategies to use. Techniques will be modeled for parents.
	2. Parents will provide Johanna with opportunities to request desired objects and activities during everyday routines. *Examples:* During play, parents will pause during tickle games to encourage Johanna to ask for more. During bathtime, parents will give Johanna a choice between a preferred and nonpreferred toy to encourage choice making. During meals, parents will give Johanna a favorite food in a tightly sealed, clear plastic jar to encourage her to ask for help.
	3. Whenever Johanna makes a request, she will receive praise and hugs along with the requested object or activity.
Johanna will play with a toy in close proximity to her brother, to prepare her for turn-taking games.	1. Preschool teacher will consult with Johanna's parents about toys Johanna plays with independently and productively at school.
	2. Parents will set up a play area by placing a blanket on the floor, select one or two preferred toys for each child, and use a kitchen timer to indicate the length of the play session. Sessions will start out brief (for example, one minute) and will be gradually increased. When the timer rings, both children will receive lots of praise and hugs, along with a special snack.
	3. Preschool teacher will use similar strategies to provide play opportunities for Johanna and a peer at school.

different sources) is provided here.[1] As you work with your IFSP team to develop a program for your child, you should try to incorporate as many of these practices as possible. This list can help you formulate thoughtful and educated questions that will guide your decisions as you put together the best possible program for your child.

Components of an Effective Treatment Program for a Young Child with Autism

- Starts intervention at a young age

- Uses assessment information to develop individualized intervention goals

- Involves families in assessment and intervention activities

- Implements teaching goals and activities that address the core deficit areas of autism: social interaction, language and communication, imitation, and play

- Provides at least twenty-five hours per week of intervention in which the child is engaged in productive activities with people or objects

- Uses a comprehensive curriculum that integrates a variety of intervention strategies

- Employs a systematic and well-planned approach to teaching

- Monitors the child's progress and reassesses goals at regular intervals

- Provides a structured and supportive teaching environment

- Incorporates activities to promote generalization of skills to other settings

- Employs a functional, proactive, and positive approach to managing and preventing problematic behaviors

By the Numbers

Autism was added as a special education exceptionality in 1991 and is now the sixth most commonly classified disability in the United States (141,022 children served). The top five most common disability classifications in 2003 were (1) specific learning disabilities (2,866,908 children served); (2) speech or language impairments (1,129,260 children served); (3) mental retardation (582,663 children served); (4) emotional disturbance (484,479 children served); and (5) other health impairments, which often includes children diagnosed with Attention-Deficit/Hyperactivity Disorder (ADHD) (452,442 children served). The number of children served under the "autism" classification for special education services is exceptionally low compared to the number of children known to be diagnosed with ASD. One of the reasons for this is that not all children with an ASD diagnosis receive special education services under the autism label, so the education data underestimate the actual prevalence of the ASDs.[2]

- Provides opportunities for structured interactions with typically developing peers
- Prepares children for transitions to future educational settings

TYPES OF EARLY INTERVENTION SERVICES

There are several types of educational services and therapies that are commonly recommended for young children with autism. Your child's IFSP team will come up with an intervention plan that will include some or all of the different service options presented in this section, so it is important that you understand what they are.

Speech-Language Therapy

Because of the language and communication deficits that are associated with autism, speech-language therapy is an important component of intervention for children with autism. Speech-language therapists typically work with children to improve their receptive language (language understanding), expressive language (use of words to communicate), articulation (enunciation of words), or a combination of these. Children with autism, in particular, often have deficits in pragmatic language (the use of language in a social context) as well, and may require intervention focused on learning such skills as getting someone's attention before talking to them, staying on topic, and using eye contact while speaking to others.

Young children with autism who have minimal language skills often also require augmentative and alternative communication (AAC) therapy approaches to learn nonverbal methods of communicating their needs and desires to others (such as signing or using pictures). A "total communication" approach that combines verbal and nonverbal approaches is often recommended for children with autism in light of the severity of their language and communication impairments.

For some children, the positive results of speech therapy open up a whole new world. This was the case for twenty-month-old Ari. His mom told me,

> At home, the only way I knew to get Ari to use words was to teach him to name the pictures I would show him on flash cards. Eventually he started labeling some pictures, but he still wasn't talking to us. But his speech-language therapist, Mary, has worked magic with him! She sets up play situations and creates activities that make him *want* to communicate with her. Yesterday she got him to say "ball" to request a ball game and "more" to get her to continue—I can't wait to try some of the same activities with him at home!

Research conducted at Vanderbilt has supported the importance of providing speech-language therapy to young children with autism.[3] We found that the number of hours of speech-language therapy children received between two and three years of age was associated with their expressive language ability at age four. Although this study doesn't provide a specific recommendation for the optimal number of hours of speech-language therapy, it does emphasize the importance of including this service in the intervention package you develop for your child.

Occupational Therapy (OT)

The goal of OT is to increase a child's independence and productivity with regard to play and self-help skills (such as feeding and dressing). Specific goals for young children with autism might be to improve fine motor skills (such as gripping a crayon or opening a Velcro fastener), eye-hand coordination (such as operating a pop-up toy or completing an inset puzzle), or self-help skills (such as using a spoon, eating a variety of foods, or pulling socks off to undress).

Because children with autism can have unusual sensory responses, some occupational therapists also offer sensory integration (SI) therapy. This therapy consists of activities designed to help children process the information they receive through their senses in a more typical manner. Examples of SI activities include brushing the child's arms with a soft-haired brush, compressing his joints, swinging him in a hammock, or having him wear a weighted vest. Despite the popularity of SI, its effectiveness for children with autism has not been studied systematically, so there is no scientific evidence that it can remediate the sensory difficulties of children with autism. Nevertheless, it is often included in intervention plans for children with autism.

Other types of OT, however, can be very helpful for many children with autism. Says the dad of three-and-a-half-year-old Caroline,

Occupational therapy was a lifesaver for our family. Mealtimes used to be a nightmare for Caroline, who refused to use utensils and would only eat chicken nuggets and a few other finger foods. Our EI service coordinator referred Caroline for an OT evaluation, and one of the recommendations in the report was that she receive OT twice per week. Her occupational therapist, Ruth, set two initial goals for Caroline: using a spoon to eat, and eating a wider variety of foods. Caroline's progress over the past two months has been phenomenal. Ruth gave her a special spoon and plate to use that makes it easier for Caroline to scoop up food, and she also gave us lots of suggestions for encouraging Caroline to use the spoon during mealtimes at home. Ruth also managed to get Caroline to eat foods with textures that she would never go near—like pudding and applesauce. Now mealtimes are one of the more peaceful routines in our home!

Physical Therapy (PT)

PT may be recommended for some children with autism who have difficulties with such gross motor skills as strength, posture, and balance. Physical therapists can help children control their movements, increase their body awareness, and develop the motor coordination required for such skills as walking, running, and jumping.

PT was especially helpful for three-year-old Mikia, whose low muscle tone affected the strength of his arms and legs. His mom says,

Even at thirty months, Mikia had difficulty climbing up on furniture, opening cabinet doors, and walking without tripping and falling down. His muscle weakness wasn't related to his autism, but his autism made it necessary to find just the right physical therapist to work with him. A parent from our local chapter of the Autism Society of America recommended a physical therapist named Jessie, and he turned out to be a great find! He and Mikia really hit it off, and somehow Jessie gets Mikia to do strengthening exercises while Mikia thinks he's playing! I've never seen resistance training that's so much fun! It turns out that Jessie has an older brother with autism, so he really likes working with kids like Mikia.

Developmental Preschool

A developmental preschool is a center-based program that is designed to serve young children with special needs or disabilities. Some programs enroll only children with disabilities; others include children with typical development as well.

Developmental preschools usually provide a comprehensive curriculum in which individualized learning objectives are taught within the context of developmentally appropriate play activities. These programs tend to have a small student-to-teacher ratio and a multidisciplinary staff that has special training in working with children with a variety of developmental disorders. Children may participate in classroom activities for partial days or full days, usually for several days per week. Often speech-language therapy, OT, and other related services are provided on-site. Some developmental preschools also have outreach programs that provide home-based interventions.

Susan is very happy that she chose a developmental preschool for her daughter. Here, two mornings a week, twenty-month-old Kaitlin has an opportunity to learn to socialize and communicate with other children under the supervision of teachers who have experience and training working with children with autism. Most of the other children in her classroom also have some type of disability, but there are still children who talk and socialize much better than Kaitlin does. The teachers are helping her learn to play near other children, to sign "more" when she wants another serving of snack, and to play with toys the way they were designed to be used. She gets lots of individual attention, and she is making great progress on her IFSP goals. "I used to worry about putting Kaitlin in a classroom where there were no typically developing peers," says Susan. "But I knew she wouldn't get the same attention from trained teachers anywhere else. To balance things out, I also bring her to a Mother's Day Out program two mornings a week, to make sure that Kaitlin also has experiences with children who have typical development."

Regular Preschool

Participation in preschool (or day-care) programs designed for typically developing young children can also be an important component of intervention for some children with autism. Community-based preschool programs offer a "natural environment" that affords children with autism the opportunity for routine exposure to and interactions with peers of about the same age. Typically developing peers can serve as behavioral models for age-appropriate social, communication, and play skills.

However, not all preschools are equipped to provide productive learning environments for children with autism. Because children with autism tend to have relatively weak imitation skills, simply being around typical peers is usually not sufficient for social learning to occur. Rather, specific teaching activities that involve both the child with autism and one or two typically developing peers need to be developed in this setting to promote interactions and teach skills. Sometimes other therapists who work with the child with autism (for example, a speech-language therapist) can arrange to come to the preschool to provide direct intervention with the child and to consult with the preschool staff regarding specific teaching activities that can be implemented.

Carlo, for example, attends a regular preschool program three mornings per week. His dad told me, "Carlo's teachers treat him just like the other kids, and we feel that it's important for him to have the same kind of preschool experiences that other children have. We want him to be around other children his age who he can learn from. But we also want to make sure that Carlo gets some specialized intervention services, so we have an ABA [applied behavior analysis, discussed in the next section] therapist come into our home two afternoons per week to work with him. This combination of preschool and in-home therapy seems to work really well for Carlo and our family."

Behavioral Intervention

Behavioral intervention has become a cornerstone of treatment for young children with autism, and ABA specifically is becoming a familiar acronym to many parents of children with autism. The term refers to *applied behavior analysis,* which is a scientific approach to the study of behavior and behavior change.

ABA is an umbrella term that comprises a variety of concepts, principles, and techniques that are used in the assessment, treatment, and prevention of problem behaviors. The goal of ABA is to increase desired behaviors and skills, decrease undesired behaviors, teach new skills, and promote generalization of newly acquired skills across home, school, and community settings. The principles of ABA have been around for a long time and apply to all human behavior, not just the behavior of children with autism. The term *ABA* is often used erroneously to refer to a specific behavioral approach advocated by Dr. Ivar Lovaas from the UCLA Clinic for the Behavioral Treatment of Children. In reality, it refers to a variety of approaches and a large body of knowledge related to the study and practice of behavior change. As a result, not all ABA programs for children with autism will be identical, though they should embrace the same general intervention philosophy.

Behavioral therapists may employ a wide range of techniques and strategies when working with children with autism. Terms associated with ABA that you may hear mentioned by therapists include *discrete trial training, incidental teaching, pivotal response training,* and the *Picture Exchange Communication System (PECS).* (Additional information about specific teaching strategies is provided in Chapter Five.) The specific ABA techniques, or combination of techniques, used should be determined after evaluating the child and identifying his or her strengths, needs, and learning style. What the different techniques have in common is their systematic approach and their emphasis on functional, measurable outcomes. The utility of ABA approaches is well supported in the research literature for children with autism as well as many other populations.

Nathan's dad, Leonard, has seen positive changes in his son since beginning ABA therapy. "At first," admits Leonard, "I didn't have much faith that these lessons would make a big difference in my son's behavior. Nathan seemed so difficult to reach and spent the first few sessions crying. But now I'm a believer! Just last week, Nathan asked for 'more' ice cream while pointing to the refrigerator. Very structured lessons that taught him little-by-little how to imitate pointing have opened up a whole new world for him."

Parent Training

Parent training is a general term that refers to services designed to help parents learn to understand, interact with, manage, and teach their children. Parent training differs from the other types of services described here in that its primary focus is on the parent, rather than on the child.

Parent training activities can take many different forms. Sometimes parent training is provided within the context of the child's therapies. For example, at the end of a speech therapy session, the therapist may show the parent how she is teaching the child to use a picture to request a snack, so that the parent can implement a similar activity at home. Sometimes parent training activities are conducted independently from other therapies; parents might, for example, participate in behavior management classes or attend a workshop to learn how to make and use visual supports for the child. Parent training activities can empower parents by improving their ability to teach their children new skills as well as to manage their behaviors.

Parent training is a critical aspect of early intervention services; unfortunately, it is often overlooked in an effort to obtain as many child-focused service hours as possible. But no one knows better than you that whereas teachers and therapists go home at the end of the day, you are tuned into your child twenty-four hours a day, seven days a week. That's why it's important that *you* know what to do with your child so you can work and play effectively with him or her within the context of the family as well as the community.

During the IFSP meeting, make sure you understand what type and combination of services are being recommended for your child. See how well the program that's recommended for your child fits with the list of effective practices provided earlier in this chapter. Also be sure to ask if the recommended services are autism-specialized and whether the service providers have experience and training in working with children with autism. *The experience and training of your service providers can be very important in determining the success of the intervention for your child.*

Unfortunately, because state EI programs have limited resources, they may not always be able to offer all the services you desire for your child. For this reason, sometimes parents decide to supplement the state-provided services with additional therapies or programs that they pay for out-of-pocket.

If you decide to explore additional therapies or programs for your child, you will soon find that the number of possibilities is overwhelming. The field of autism is rife with different types of interventions, many claiming to be the "best" or "only" way to help your child. The next sections provide some suggestions for how to sort through the numerous treatment options that you will encounter as you start to do your own research. We will look at two categories of treatments: "brand-name" programs and complementary and alternative therapies.

"BRAND-NAME" PROGRAMS

There are several "brand-name" programs for children with autism that are particularly popular among parents who choose to pay for private therapies. Unfortunately, I can't tell you that any one program

♡ PARENTS SAY
Thoughts About Early Intervention

- The lack of information at the time of diagnosis about what these kids can possibly achieve in the future can leave a parent in a heap on the floor. But then the therapists were the first ones to say that we could make progress and my child could learn. These were things I already knew in my heart, but I just needed to hear a professional say so out loud. They didn't have to give me definites or parameters. I just needed that confirmation of hope and the potential for progress. (mother of nine-year-old boy)

- Don't wait to start intervention. I am hopeful that autism can be curable if you intervene early and redirect brain growth when the child is still a toddler. (father of three-year-old girl diagnosed at twenty-seven months)

- I had compiled a binder full of possible treatments to try with my son. So many possibilities, but no guaranteed outcomes. I'm so glad the doctor took away all that confusion by giving me a detailed list explaining exactly what I needed to do to help my son. (mother of twenty-four-month-old boy diagnosed at nineteen months)

- Early intervention helps so much. In seventeen months, my son has gone from being almost nonverbal to constantly talking. His speech therapist says that sometimes she even has to tell him to wait his turn to talk! (mother of four-year-old boy diagnosed at thirty-three months) will be the best for your child. They all have different philosophies and employ different approaches, and because of the various ways autism affects different children, no one program will be right for everyone. Family styles differ as well. Some parents are more comfortable with a structured or "drill and practice" approach, whereas others prefer an approach that is more heavily rooted in play or in relationship building. As you wade through this information, keep these two important facts in mind:

1. *No "brand" of early intervention program has been proven to be superior to another.*

2. *No single intervention will be "right" for every child with autism.*

Please memorize these two facts and keep repeating them to yourself as you continue your search. In a way, they can make choosing an intervention program even harder for you. Without one ideal program that stands above all others, you have to choose among various programs that can be equally successful in helping your child learn. The best way to make that difficult choice is to (1) understand the components of effective interventions that were listed earlier, (2) consider the unique needs of your child and the rest of your family, and (3) get as much information about each program as you can. Because no two children with autism are alike, just as no two families are alike, the intervention that another family chooses may not be the right one for you. I have provided a form "Questions to Ask About Autism Treatments" (Figure 4.1) to help you gather specific information about different treatments and therapy programs; doing so will help you make an educated and informed decision.

On this form you will find questions that cover several important aspects of early intervention. You need to know about the program itself, about the therapists, and about your own involvement. You should find out what the goals will be and how progress will be measured. It's also vital to know how the therapist will work with

FIGURE 4.1. Questions to Ask About Autism Treatments.

Program: _____

Location: _____

Hrs/wk: _____   Cost: _____

CONTENT OF PROGRAM

Which area(s) of development does your treatment focus on?
(e.g., language, communication, toy play, imitation, peer play,
social interactions, behavior, preacademic skills, work skills, parent
training)

How will you identify specific goals for my child?

How will you determine which behaviors/skills to begin with?

What approach(es) will you use to teach my child?

What approach(es) will you use to manage my child's behavior?

MEASURING PROGRESS

**How will I know if my child is making progress? What types of
improvements should I expect?**

How long will it be before I see changes?

**How will *you* know if my child is making progress? How will you
measure progress? What will you use?**

How often will you assess progress?

What will happen if my child doesn't improve with this treatment?

THERAPIST QUALIFICATIONS

How many children with autism have you worked with? _____
What ages? _____

Do you also serve children over three years old?

What are your qualifications? What type of training do you have?

Do you have a professional degree or certificate? (if so, get specifics)

Are you affiliated with a professional organization? (if so, get specifics)

What do you see as your strongest skills in working with children
with autism?

How is working with children with autism different from working
with other children?

What kinds of issues or problems would you consider to be *outside*
your realm of expertise?

SCIENTIFIC EVIDENCE OF EFFECTIVENESS

Is there research to support the effectiveness of this type of
treatment? (get details as well as copies of published articles)

FIGURE 4.1. Questions to Ask About Autism Treatments, *continued.*

Has research shown this treatment to be *better than* other types of treatment?

PROFESSIONAL INVOLVEMENT

Who will be providing the direct intervention with my child?

What type of training do they have?

Who will be supervising them? How will supervision be conducted?

How often will *you* see my child?

PARENT INVOLVEMENT

Will I be able to participate in the treatment?

Will you teach *me* to work with my child? How?

What types of skills will you teach me? (get examples)

COMPATIBILITY WITH OTHER TREATMENTS

How many hours per week of your treatment will my child need?

Is your treatment compatible with other interventions my child is participating in?

How do you collaborate with other service providers who are working with my child? (get examples) other therapists who may be treating your child. And you certainly have a right to know *what kind* of research has been conducted on this therapy or treatment and what the results were.

Make several copies of Figure 4.1. Then carefully identify on the top of each form the specific therapy being evaluated and get the answers to each question. This will give you the objective information you need to be sure that the early intervention your child receives has a strong track record of helping young children with autism.

Whether or not you decide to pursue any of the following treatment options, it's important to be familiar with them so you will have a working vocabulary of the specific terms used in this new world of autism of which you are now officially a member. I've offered this quick peek at the most common interventions (presented in alphabetical order) so that you will have a basic understanding of their methods and theoretical underpinnings and will be in a better position to explore and pursue the programs you believe will be best for your child and family.

Developmental, Individual-Difference, Relationship-Based (DIR) Model/Floortime

The DIR model was developed by Drs. Stanley Greenspan and Serena Wieder. It is based on the theory that children with autism experience a variety of biological challenges in the areas of sensory processing and motor planning that make it difficult for them to interact, communicate, and learn. DIR fosters the emotional development of the child using a relationship-based model in which parents and other adults interact with the child in specific ways to enhance his or her social-emotional, communicative, and cognitive development.

"Floortime" is an essential component of this approach. It is a twenty- to thirty-minute period in which a parent gets down on the floor with the child and plays with him by following his lead, elaborating his play, and establishing a warm and positive interaction.

Scientific, controlled studies on the effectiveness of the DIR/floortime approach have not yet been conducted.

Early Intensive Behavior Intervention (EIBI)

This approach, developed by Dr. Ivar Lovaas, involves the use of a specific ABA technique—discrete trial training—that is conducted in an intensive, forty-hour-per-week program.

Discrete trial training is conducted in a one-on-one setting with an adult and is designed to increase skills and improve behaviors. It involves breaking down skills into individual (discrete) components and teaching one component at a time in a highly structured manner. Each trial consists of three steps that occur in rapid succession: the adult gives an instruction (such as "Point to the circle"), the child responds (either correctly or incorrectly), and the adult provides immediate feedback (such as "That's right" or "Try again"). Each teaching episode involves the repetition of many discrete trials. Research findings support the use of discrete trial training as a teaching tool; however, initial research findings of dramatic improvements for children participating in EIBI have not been replicated by other scientists to date.

Relationship Development Intervention (RDI)

RDI is a parent-based treatment that was developed by Dr. Steven Gutstein and first introduced in 2001. RDI is designed to improve the quality of life of children with autism by addressing deficits such as rigid thinking and difficulty understanding the thoughts and feelings of others. The focus is on giving children the motivation and tools for sharing experiences with others and for interacting successfully with friends and family. Goals include the development of empathy, flexible thinking, and creative problem solving. There are currently no scientific, controlled studies assessing the effectiveness of the RDI model.

Structured Teaching

The structured teaching approach was developed at TEACCH (Treatment and Education of Autistic and Related Communication Handicapped Children), a statewide program founded in 1972 by Dr. Eric Schopler and based at the University of North Carolina. This program emphasizes the individualized assessment of children's strengths, interests, needs, and learning styles, and the implementation of developmentally appropriate activities to promote skill acquisition and independent functioning.

Structured teaching is a major component of TEACCH philosophy, and refers to a system that capitalizes on the strengths in visual learning that are characteristic of autism. Structured teaching creates a visually clear and organized environment that serves to communicate expectations and increase predictability for children with autism. Structured teaching techniques include the use of physical boundaries to separate different activity areas, visual schedules to convey the sequence of activities, and other forms of visual supports to promote success, develop organizational skills, and foster independence. Research has supported the use of structured teaching approaches for children with autism.

COMPLEMENTARY AND ALTERNATIVE TREATMENTS

In addition to the various state-funded and private learning programs available to children with autism, there are also innumerable alternative treatments available—these are often called CAM, which stands for *complementary and alternative medicine*. The term CAM refers to medical and health care practices and products that are not currently considered part of standard medical care or procedures. Some CAM therapies are used as an adjunct to conventional health care; others are used in place of more conventional treatments.

Although there are many different types of CAM therapies, they all share one thing in common: *a lack of scientific evidence supporting their safety or their effectiveness in treating the symptoms and conditions for which they are used.* For some treatments, no rigorous scientific studies have yet been completed; for others, research has been conducted, but conflicting findings prevent definitive conclusions; and for still others, research has consistently failed to demonstrate positive treatment effects.

Yet CAM therapies are growing in popularity. In fact, it's believed that as many as 30 to 50 percent of children with autism in the United States may be receiving some type of complementary or alternative treatment.[4]

There are several possible reasons for the increased popularity of scientifically unproven treatments. One is that they often offer the promise of a cure. For a disorder like autism, which at the present time has no identified cause and no known cure, this promise can give parents a sense of optimism and hope that may not be available elsewhere.

Another reason for the appeal of alternative therapies is the type of media coverage they often receive. Television stories about dramatic treatment responses to new therapies attract the interest and attention of viewers (as well as sponsors). Personal testimonials from parents who are in a situation similar to yours can be very compelling, even if they are presented in the absence of scientific evidence.

Finally, the accessibility of the Internet has increased our exposure to the myriad unproven treatments that are promoted through the use of sophisticated marketing techniques, rather than through research-based evidence of their effectiveness.

If you choose to explore CAM options, please move forward with care. There's no doubt that you want to give your child every possible advantage and opportunity, and you're probably open to anything that holds out promise of improvement. But that shouldn't make you less cautious about your child's health and his or her needs. These treatments can be quite costly, and some have been associated with serious negative side effects. Just because a treatment is touted as "natural" doesn't mean that it's safe, so you can't let your optimism overrule common sense. You should not, for example, take your child out of speech therapy so you can afford an unproven alternative treatment, such as heavy metal detoxification.

If you do decide to try an alternative treatment of any kind, keep these two guidelines in mind:

1. Bring your child's pediatrician into the loop. Even if he or she disagrees with your thoughts or decisions, you must be open and honest so that you can be made aware of any possible side effects or drug interactions that might occur. Your child's pediatrician may also be able to guide you to the safest form of the intervention you choose and help you monitor your child's progress along the way.

2. Read the section that appears later in this chapter that explains the scientific method for evaluating the effectiveness of treatments. It will assist you in making sound decisions that are more likely to help than hurt your child.

A sampling of CAM options that are advertised for children with autism is provided in the following sections. I have not gone into great detail describing each one because there is insufficient evidence that any of them work to improve the symptoms of autism—that's why they're called "alternative." These are some of the more popular alternative treatments being talked about today, but you and I both know that tomorrow there may be something brand new making the rounds of Internet chat rooms and claiming superiority over all other programs.

Dietary Supplements

Dietary supplements are among the most commonly used of the CAM therapies. The theory underlying their use is that children with autism are deficient in certain biochemicals that are important for optimal brain functioning or immune responses. The suggested doses of these supplements generally are higher than the recommended daily allowance, and information regarding their long-term side effects is limited. The specific ingredients in supplements are not regulated by the FDA, so they may vary across commercially available brands or even across batches from the same company. Please approach them with caution.

Vitamin B$_6$ and Magnesium.   Vitamin B$_6$ (pyridoxine) plays a vital role in synthesizing important neurotransmitters, such as serotonin and gamma-aminobutyric acid (GABA). Some believe that vitamin B$_6$ along with magnesium (which is needed to make vitamin B$_6$ effective) can decrease behavioral problems, improve eye contact and attention span, and improve learning ability. However, side effects of this treatment can include hyperactivity and irritability. In addition, long-term doses of B$_6$ have been associated with peripheral neuropathy, which causes tingling in hands and feet.

Vitamin C.   Vitamin C (ascorbic acid) is involved in the synthesis of neurotransmitters, in addition to acting as an antioxidant and a regulator of cellular immune function. It is thought to relieve symptoms of autism, especially stereotyped behaviors. High doses can cause gastrointestinal upset (including diarrhea) or possibly kidney stones.

Vitamin A.   Vitamin A occurs naturally in cod liver oil and is involved in augmenting the body's immune response. Some believe that the specific immune response modulated by vitamin A is disrupted by the MMR vaccine and that vitamin A therapy can counteract this problem. High doses of vitamin A (such as those found in one teaspoon of some preparations of cod liver oil) can cause a number of serious side effects, especially in young children.

Dimethylglycine (DMG).   DMG is a food supplement that is thought to be involved with neurotransmitter synthesis and with immune function enhancement. It has been reported to improve language and behavior in children with autism, though systematic clinical trial research has not found DMG to be more effective than a placebo (a supplement not containing DMG) in reducing the symptoms of autism.

Fatty Acids. It is thought that essential fatty acids and omega-3 fatty acids are involved in the production of prostaglandins, which can affect the functioning of the brain and other systems. A controlled research study with children with ADHD did not reveal fatty acid supplementation to reduce clinical symptoms. Comparable research with children with autism has not been conducted.

Elimination Diets

The most common elimination diet used to treat children with autism is the gluten-free and casein-free (GF-CF) diet. This diet arose from the belief that autism is caused by a poorly functioning gastrointestinal system. Some feel that children with autism have a "leaky gut" syndrome that leads to an inability to completely break down such proteins as gluten (which is found in products containing wheat, oats, barley, and rye) and casein (which is found in cow's milk and other dairy products). The hypothesis regarding the link between the leaky gut and autism is that fragments of the partially digested food proteins are absorbed into the system and act as opioids, which cause such symptoms as decreased social interaction, repetitive behaviors, decreased sensitivity to pain, and impaired learning. It is thought that the GF-CF diet will thus improve the symptoms of autism by restricting the intake of the improperly digested proteins.

At this point there is little scientific evidence to support either the underlying theory about the leaky gut-autism link or the GF-CF diet itself. Issues of proper nutrition, as well as the cost and difficulty of maintaining this diet, should be considered prior to starting this treatment.

Biological Agents

Biological agents that are used to treat other medical conditions, such as multiple sclerosis, digestive problems, and lead poisoning, have been used experimentally to treat children with autism. The three most common treatments in this category that you'll surely hear about as you research early interventions are intravenous immunoglobulin, chelation, and secretin.

Intravenous Immunoglobulin (IV-IG). Intravenous immunoglobulin is a plasma-derived product that is used to treat several neurological disorders (such as multiple sclerosis) that are thought to be caused by immune deficiencies. Its use has been extended to autism based on the theory that immune system abnormalities or deficiencies are also present in, and may cause, autism. Systematic scientific studies on IV-IG have not been conducted, and some side effects of this treatment have been reported.

Chelation/Heavy Metal Detoxification. The process of chelation involves the administration of specific drugs to remove heavy metals or other toxins from the body. Excess heavy metals can interfere with brain and other systemic functions. Chelation has been used to reduce lead levels in individuals who have dangerously high levels of lead in their bloodstream. The use of chelation for children with autism stems from the belief that autism is caused by abnormally high levels of mercury that accumulate in body tissues as a result of early childhood vaccinations containing thimerosal.

The most common chelating agent used is dimercaptosuccinic acid (DMSA). Mercury chelation treatment is especially controversial because (1) mercury is no longer used in childhood vaccines in the United States, (2) many large-scale studies have failed to show a link between thimerosal and autism, and (3) DMSA can have harsh side effects, including abdominal pain and liver toxicity.

Secretin. Secretin therapy is one of the best examples of how a dramatic media report can lead to widespread use of a treatment before its effectiveness has been studied systematically by researchers. Several years ago, a national TV news magazine show reported on three children with autism whose symptoms resolved after receiving secretin during diagnostic testing (endoscopy) for digestive problems. (Secretin is a gastrointestinal hormone used to assess functioning of the pancreas.) The anecdotal reports and parent testimonials on the show led thousands of parents to seek secretin treatment for their children. Since that time, numerous well-controlled clinical trial studies have been conducted and published in scientific journals (which involves rigorous review by other experts in the field). Consistently, the results have not supported the hype; secretin is no more effective than placebo in improving the symptoms of autism. It is ironic that an ineffective therapy like secretin ended up being one of the most carefully studied and well-investigated treatments for any childhood disorder.

Other Alternative Therapies

If you search the Web with the keywords "CAM and autism," you'll find over seventy-five thousand hits. Obviously, there are many people out there who think they have found the cure, and I can't begin to cover them all here. The only additional two alternative therapies that I would like to mention are Auditory Integration Training and Facilitated Communication. These are therapies that you are likely to run across in your search and therefore you certainly should know the basics.

Auditory Integration Training (AIT). AIT was developed by Dr. Guy Berard, a French otolaryngologist, to treat individuals with auditory processing difficulties, particularly sound hypersensitivity. This procedure involves the repeated exposure to different sounds through earphones to "retrain" the ear and improve the way the brain processes auditory information. The underlying theory is that distortions in hearing or auditory processing may contribute to behavioral and learning problems. Although claims of improved language, attention, social interactions, and academic performance following treatment have been reported, controlled scientific studies have not supported these claims. AIT is not endorsed by the American Academy of Pediatrics.

Facilitated Communication (FC). FC is a specific method of communication in which a child types out messages on a keyboard or other communication device while a "facilitator" supports the child's hand, often using a hand-over-hand position. The theory underlying this treatment is that severe motor problems prevent children with autism from learning more conventional methods of communication and that even individuals with severe mental retardation have normal communication and cognitive potential. FC is hypothesized to provide a means for children with autism to express their true abilities as well as their inner feelings, sometimes through poetry or intellectual conversations. Systematic, controlled research on FC has failed to provide evidence for the effectiveness of this treatment. In fact, results reveal that much of the communication originates from the facilitator rather than the child. In light of these consistent findings, several professional organizations, including the American Association on Mental Retardation, the American Academy of Child and Adolescent Psychiatry, the American Speech-Language-Hearing Association, and the American Psychological Association, have adopted a formal position of opposing FC.

EVALUATING AUTISM TREATMENTS

This chapter has explored just some of the therapies and treatments available for children with autism. Some may become part of your child's state EI program; others may be part of private therapy you will choose for your child; still others may be treatments you've heard of or read about and are considering trying yourself. But which ones are the best? This is a question I get almost every day from parents, and unfortunately, I can't answer it—no one can.

We just don't know at this time which interventions work "best" with which symptoms of autism in which children. We do know, however, that some have proven their effectiveness over and over again in research studies that use the scientific method of evaluation—these are the therapies and treatments you should focus on during this time of exploration so that you don't get tangled up in treatments that take advantage of your vulnerability.

The Scientific Method

The scientific method is used to study a phenomenon in an objective, unbiased manner. It helps researchers and scientists distinguish between facts and beliefs. For example, if I feel a cold coming on, I might take a tablet containing the herb Echinacea. If I don't have a cold the next day, it would be easy for me to believe that the Echinacea cured my symptoms. But that might not be the true explanation. Instead, my symptoms might have improved because I went to bed earlier that evening and got more rest, because I drank lots of liquids, or because my scratchy throat was not really signaling a cold but instead was an allergic response that later subsided on its own. The only way to tell whether Echinacea works to prevent cold symptoms is to use the scientific method to study its effectiveness in a careful, systematic, controlled manner that allows us to rule out other possible causes for symptom improvement.

We can think of autism treatments in a similar way. If Ben's parents add vitamin A supplements to his diet and see improvement, they may believe that this treatment was the cause of his improvement. If they then hear success stories from other parents on a news program or in a chat room, they may feel more confident that the treatment was responsible for Ben's improvements. They may become totally convinced that the treatment works after reading on a Web site that ten children in a "study" using this same treatment showed improvement in their symptoms. Although this treatment might in fact be responsible for Ben's improvements, we really don't have enough information to know for sure.

That's because we know only part of the story—we know only about the treatment successes. The success stories are the ones that make news. We don't know how many children used the treatment and *didn't* improve, nor do we know how many children *didn't* use the treatment and improved anyway.

For example, Ben's parents may become less enthusiastic about the treatment's effectiveness if they find out that there were a total of fifty children in that "study" in which the ten children improved.

It may be even more discouraging for them to learn that in another group of fifty children who *didn't* use the treatment, thirty improved. (The list that follows summarizes the results of this study.) These numbers suggest that more children improved *without* the treatment than *with* it! Although this is a very simplified example, I hope it illustrates the point that we need information about children in all four quadrants of this list in order to make educated decisions about treatment options.

	Used Treatment	Didn't Use Treatment
Improved	10	30
Didn't improve	40	20
Total	50	50

There is no way we can know whether or not an intervention works until we put it to the scientific test. Research studies must be designed in a specific way to ensure that any improvements that are found are due to the treatment itself, rather than caused by factors that are not specific to the treatment. For example, one of the most well-known, nonspecific treatment effects is the placebo effect. The placebo effect is an amazing phenomenon that has been demonstrated over and over again: if we simply *expect* or believe that a treatment will work, we will often experience symptom improvement. (For young children involved in treatment, the placebo effect applies to the parent rather than the child.)

No one knows exactly how or why the placebo effect works—but I bet some of you have made a doctor's appointment because you didn't feel well and then started feeling better shortly after making the appointment. It's the same phenomenon: the hope and expectation of a cure can make us feel better.

When we design a scientific study, the placebo effect must be investigated as well. For example, if a dietary supplement is given in the form of a powder, then some children in the study would have to get the same powder, but without the supplement. Neither the child nor the family can know whether the supplement or placebo was given—this is what is known as a "blind" study. In this way, we can make an unbiased and objective determination about the effects of the treatment.

The Cautious Approach

It is only through the use of carefully designed experiments that we can tell whether an intervention really works. Some researchers study the effectiveness of treatments using *group design* studies. In this type of study, a group of children who receive the treatment (the experimental group) is compared to a group who do not (the control group). The experimental and control groups are similar on as many dimensions as possible prior to the treatment, so that any group differences that are found following treatment are likely to be due to the treatment itself, rather than to differences between the groups of children. In most cases, the control group will receive a different treatment rather than no treatment at all, so that parents of children in both groups will have similar expectations for improvement. It is important that children be randomly assigned to the different treatments; doing so helps ensure that the groups are similar on nontreatment factors.

Other researchers use *single-case* designs, in which a small number of children are studied intensively through direct observation over an extended period of time. Specific behaviors are observed during baseline (no intervention) and treatment conditions, which are manipulated systematically. Differences in behavior patterns observed during baseline and treatment are examined to determine the treatment's effectiveness.

Specific standards have been established for designing and interpreting research studies to determine an intervention's effectiveness.[5] Treatments that meet certain criteria are considered to be *empirically validated* or *evidence-based* treatments. As a rule of thumb, evidence from ten single-case design studies demonstrating the effectiveness of an intervention is required for the intervention to be considered validated. For group design studies, two studies in which the intervention is found to be superior to an alternative one are required. For both types of studies, evidence of treatment effectiveness must be obtained by different research groups, to ensure that the findings can be replicated by scientists located at different institutions and using different samples.

You can see that scientific method is not easy or quick. It does not allow one to jump to conclusions or spread false hope. It is methodical, exact, and consistent because your child's health depends on its findings. Knowing how true research works, you can be more skeptical of treatments that are touted to be "proven effective." Ben's parents may have been curious about the study that showed symptom improvement in ten children, but they were also smart enough to find out how many children didn't show improvement. They also knew that the positive findings could have been the result of other factors (such as children's maturation or another therapy the children were receiving at the same time) that were not monitored during the study.

Now you too know why you must be so cautious. There are many therapies and treatments out there for autism that feed off parents' desperation and their willingness to blindly buy into an intervention simply because it offers hope. For the sake of your child's future, which depends on appropriate early intervention, you must make your decisions based on sound scientific knowledge.

Quick Elimination List

For starters, you can use a quick process of elimination[6] by being immediately cautious of any treatment that

- Offers a cure for autism

- Promises to be effective for all children

- Claims to improve all the symptoms of autism

- Requires you to suspend your belief system and adopt that of the treatment's promoters (for example, asks you to "believe" in things that don't make common sense, or tells you that the treatment won't work unless you believe in it)

- Consists of a general package or predetermined curriculum that is not tailored to the needs of the individual child

- Does not provide routine and periodic assessments of the child's progress and the treatment's effectiveness

- Claims to be "the best" treatment for your child or "the only" treatment your child needs

Any program or treatment that is still in the running after you have scrutinized it using the information and questions provided throughout this chapter can then move on to more serious consideration.

A STORY OF EARLY DETECTION: PART THREE

Luke's mother, Judy, continues the family's story.

> Well, Jeff and I thought learning about Luke's diagnosis would be the hardest part of this whole process, but little did we know how hard it would be to figure out the next step! The first thing I did when I got home was start looking up

RESEARCH TODAY

There have been thousands of valid studies trying to find a scientifically sound basis for the positive experiences some have had with as-yet-unproven alternative medicine. In fact, the government has created a Web site addressing the value and influence of CAM on modern medical practices, while at the same time explaining the reasons for caution and patience. If you are interested in alternative therapies, do your own research with care and vigilance and be sure to visit the Web site of the National Center for Complementary and Alternative Medicine (http://nccam.nih.gov). Here you will find valuable information, including a discussion of this list of questions that you should consider when evaluating information you read about CAM on Web sites:[7]

1. Who runs this site?

2. Who pays for the site?

3. Where does the information come from?

4. How is the information reviewed and selected?

5. How current is the information?

6. How does the site choose links to other sites?

7. What information about you does the site collect and why?

information about autism and autism treatments on the Internet. To be honest, I consider myself to be a pretty Internet-savvy person, but I was absolutely lost trying to sort through all the information I came across that day. I cried myself to sleep that night in sheer desperation and panic. Luckily the psychologist had given me the phone number for the local chapter of the Autism Society of America and I already had my contact, Stacie, at the state EI agency, so I was able to call them both the next day and was quickly pointed in the right direction.

The person at the Autism Society gave me the names and phone numbers of other parents of young children with autism. I knew I might want to contact them at some point, but I definitely wasn't ready yet—I was sure that once I started talking to them I would cry uncontrollably. I also learned from that phone call that the Autism Society has an orientation meeting once a month for families of newly diagnosed children, so Jeff and I talked about going to the next one if we were feeling brave enough. The person on the phone was also a parent, and she suggested that I buy a notebook so that I could keep all of Luke's information in one place, and that turned out to be good advice.

At that point, I hadn't told my parents yet about Luke's diagnosis. I was afraid that they wouldn't believe the evaluation results and would want us to get a second opinion, when all I wanted to do at that point was move forward and come up with a plan for him. I thought it might be better to wait until I could also explain to them what kind of therapies Luke would be getting.

When I called Stacie at the EI program, she explained about the IFSP process, she told me she would start setting up the IFSP meeting, now that all the evaluations had been completed, and we talked about who should be invited. I asked her for some clues about what types of services Luke might get now that he had the official diagnosis (so I could start reading about them), but she said she wouldn't know until the IFSP team met. So I was back in familiar territory—waiting!!

The IFSP meeting went well, and we ended up with a treatment plan that continued the speech-language therapy twice a week and the occupational therapy once a week. We added behavioral intervention three times a week and parent training once a week. Altogether Luke would be getting about ten hours per week, and all of the therapies would take place at our home. I had read that twenty-five hours per week was recommended, so I asked if we could get more therapy time, but Stacie said that the EI program could provide only this level of service to start out with. I didn't have the energy to argue, especially because all these services were free, but decided that I was ready to talk to other parents to see what kind of treatments they had arranged for their children.

We went to the Autism Society meeting, and everyone there seemed very supportive and willing to help us any way they could. But because each child with autism is not exactly like any other child with autism, each family was using a different combination of therapies that they thought were best for their child—but I had no idea what would work best for Luke. I left the meeting feeling optimistic, but still uncertain about how to get the best treatment for my son. I decided to see how Luke would do with the program that had been set up by Stacie and the others, and look into additional services later if it became necessary. That was the first time I felt like we were finally moving forward with a plan.

FREQUENTLY ASKED QUESTIONS

My two-year-old son is nonverbal, and his speech therapist wants to teach him to use pictures to communicate. If he becomes dependent on pictures, won't that prevent him from developing speech?

Absolutely not! There is no evidence that teaching children nonverbal methods of communication will interfere with their acquisition of language. Children who don't yet use language need to have *some* way to convey their desires to others, and nonverbal methods give them the ability to communicate. Children without autism who have language delays are able to use gestures to get their needs met. But the development of gestures is also often impaired in young children with autism, which can leave them with *no* way to communicate. This can be extremely frustrating for the child (and parent!) and may contribute to behavioral difficulties.

One method for teaching nonverbal children with autism to communicate is called the Picture Exchange Communication System, or PECS. PECS was developed by Dr. Andy Bondy and Lori Frost, and is a structured, sequenced program based on ABA principles. Children are taught to give picture symbols to an adult in order to receive a desired object. Research indicates that PECS can foster the development of spoken language as well as improve behavior problems.

How long and how often should the intervention sessions be?

There is no magic combination of services or number of hours of intervention that all children should have. However, based on reviews of the literature, it is recommended that young children with autism receive at least twenty-five hours per week of "directed intervention," which is time spent engaged in productive activity. Directed intervention may be provided in individual or group formats, at home or in school, by parents or professionals.

I know some older children with autism who are taking medications to help control their symptoms. My doctor hasn't even mentioned this possibility to me. Would medication help?

Pharmacological (medication) therapy is not commonly used for young children with autism. Most medications have not been tested in very young children, so their safety and long-term effects are unknown. Although older children with autism may take medications to increase attention, reduce anxiety, or decrease repetitive behaviors, these types of medications are rarely a routine part of a young child's treatment regimen.

❧

With answers in hand to the questions on the form "Questions to Ask About Autism Treatments," you will finally have what you need to make the best decision possible regarding appropriate early intervention for your child. Now, when you evaluate your child's IFSP and consider choosing additional interventions, you can feel satisfied in your heart that you have done everything you could have done for your child's developmental growth—well, almost everything. In the next chapter, you will learn how you yourself can enhance the benefits of your child's intervention program. There are many games, activities, and daily practices that target specific needs of children with autism that you can learn to use in your daily life with your child. You can now hush that nagging cry that says, "I wish there was something I could do." Now there is. Read on!

5

WORKING WITH YOUR CHILD AT HOME

Getting your child the appropriate services as outlined in Chapter Four isn't always an easy job. But once your child starts early intervention, the therapists will work with him or her to improve social interactions, language and communication skills, and play skills. Ideally your child's unique profile of abilities and needs will drive the therapy sessions, and each therapist will tailor the interventions to address your child's specific deficits. This early attention is the key to improving developmental delays.

Also key is your continued involvement. Your child needs your help to apply all that he or she is learning to home activities and family relationships. Children with autism often have difficulty generalizing new skills to different situations, so it can be very helpful to provide instruction in different settings. Therefore, the therapists should give you ideas for how to carry over teaching techniques, goals, and activities to the home environment.

In some programs, the child's parents are brought into the action right away. They are taught how to continue the therapy at home and are given careful instruction on how to help their children use their new skills in their daily lives when interacting with family members. Other programs give parents very little or no information about their role in their children's therapy, so parents may assume their children are getting all they need during their therapy sessions. This is unfortunate, because the more practice and reinforcement the child can have at home, the more likely he or she is to show improvement.

In this chapter, I've put together some suggestions for activities you can do with your child at home. These activities focus on improving skills in four areas that are often difficult for young children with autism:

1. Social interaction

2. Communication (requesting and joint attention)

3. Functional play

4. Imitation

Please note, however, that these activities should not be used *instead of* professional therapy—they should be thought of as complements to your child's other interventions. In fact, I suggest that you show these activities to your child's therapists and ask if they are compatible with the approach the therapists are using. If not, ask for ideas about how the activities can be "tweaked" so that you can work with your child at home to support his or her development. It's important to let each therapist know that you are open to working with your child and that you expect to be considered part of his or her therapy team.

If you're reading this chapter before your child's delays have been officially evaluated and diagnosed, go ahead and try any activities you like. Whether your child is ultimately diagnosed with autism or not, these activities cannot hurt and may certainly help.

TEACHING STRATEGIES

Before we get started with the activities, I want to give you some general teaching strategies for young children with autism that we use at our TRIAD clinic at Vanderbilt Kennedy Center and Vanderbilt Children's Hospital. This information is important because it gives you a framework for understanding and implementing the activities that follow. There are three sections of introductory material: (1) combining different teaching methods, (2) identifying and using rewards, and (3) using prompts. These will provide the foundation on which you'll build your at-home teaching activities.

Combining Different Teaching Methods

When TRIAD clinicians work with families, we use an integrated approach that incorporates different kinds of teaching methods. We employ a combination of adult-directed teaching methods (such as those used in discrete trial training), child-directed teaching methods (such as those used in incidental teaching), and visual supports (such as those used in structured teaching). I do not expect you to become an expert in each of these different teaching methodologies from reading this book. However, I've found in my work with families that different children respond better to certain teaching methods (or combinations of strategies) and that some parents are more comfortable using some methods than others. I therefore want to increase your familiarity with these different methods so that you can choose whichever combination feels best to you.

Adult-Directed Teaching.   During adult-directed teaching, you are the only one who decides what the activity will be, when and where it will occur, and which materials you will use. Behaviors are taught one at a time, in small, separate steps. This method can be especially effective for teaching brand-new skills.

For example, you may want Charles to learn to operate a pop-up toy (the kind that has different types of switches that make different cartoon characters pop out from under their lids) so that he can play more productively and entertain himself for short periods of time. You've seen him play briefly with this toy before, but he operates only one of the switches before moving on to something else. You decide to have a teaching session with this toy after breakfast, while sitting with him at his play table.

In its simplest form, adult-directed teaching follows a specific sequence:

1. You give the child a specific instruction (such as "Push the button.").

2. The child responds in one way or another (pushes the button and activates the pop-up, tries to push the button, or ignores you and does something else).

3. You provide feedback to the child (saying perhaps "Great job!" or "Try again!").

If Charles is not successful, you can provide a physical prompt (described later in the chapter) after giving the instruction. In the example of the pop-up toy, an appropriate prompt might be to gently guide his hand toward the button. This sequence is repeated until Charles is able to push the button consistently on request—this may take five minutes or two weeks, depending on the child. After he has mastered pushing the button, you can then teach him to operate the other switches on the toy, one at a time.

For this type of teaching, it's helpful to choose a toy in which the child has shown some interest, and it's *critical* to select a toy that he or she is physically capable of operating. It's also good to keep the work area free from distractions, to keep the verbal instructions brief, and to use the same verbal instruction during each trial. It can also be helpful to give tangible or physical rewards (such as a small food treat or a quick tickle) in addition to the verbal praise (as explained more fully in the next section).

As your child achieves mastery, it's important to generalize this skill to other situations. For example, you can have the teaching session occur on the floor in his room, have his sister work with him at the table, or use a different pop-up toy that is similar but not identical to the original one. In each case, the adult-directed sequence of instruction, response, and feedback stays the same.

Child-Directed Teaching. During child-directed teaching, you follow the child's lead and introduce teaching opportunities during activities that the child has chosen and is engaged in. For example, if Maria is sitting on the floor rolling a toy car, you can take another toy car, roll it near hers, and then when she is watching, demonstrate a different action with the car that will expand the variety of her play. You can say "Look what I can do!" and then roll the car down a ramp or roll it into a tower of blocks so they all come tumbling down. Again, you will give Maria lots of positive reinforcement if she imitates your play action (or even watches your activity with the toy!).

Your role is less directive with this teaching approach. Instead of giving your child instructions, you play alongside her, imitate her actions with toys, and demonstrate new ways to play. Imitating the play of young children with autism is a good way to develop their imitation skills as well as their interactive turn-taking skills. When Maria is aware that you are doing the same thing with a similar toy, she may repeat her action and then watch to see whether you do it again. This is the beginning of a good back-and-forth interaction. Sometimes instead of copying Maria's action exactly, you can change it a little and see if she will imitate the change. She may even change *her* action to see if you will copy the new action. This back-and-forth attention to her own actions and yours is an important part of establishing positive social interactions.

One of the advantages of child-directed activities is that they can occur anywhere, anytime—all you have to do is be on the lookout for teaching opportunities! Opportunities to expand Maria's toy play or imitation skills may arise when she is playing with toys in the bathtub or when she is playing with a shovel in the sandbox at the park. Opportunities to expand her communication may occur when she shows interest in getting a toy that's out of reach or when she is having trouble opening the wrapping on a favorite snack. These are times you can teach her appropriate ways to communicate her needs and desires, and then reward her by letting her have the object of her interest. (Specific ideas for teaching communication skills with this method are presented later.)

Teaching with Visual Supports.   Visual supports are used to convey information to children about what we expect them to do.

They enable children with autism to use their strengths in visual perception to compensate for their relative weaknesses in language understanding and expression. For example, young children with autism may not understand when you say, "Go into the family room and play with your trucks, but do not turn on the TV" or "After we pick up Jannie from school today, we have to stop at the drug store instead of coming straight home." However, this type of information can be conveyed through symbols and pictures that the child can be taught to use. For example, the placement of a small rug can be used to define the area in which the child is expected to play, and a picture of a stop sign on the TV can indicate that it is off-limits during a certain period of time. The usual schedule for picking up Jannie might include pictures (from left to right) of the house, the car, Jannie's school, and the house again. On days when there is a detour, a picture of the extra activity (such as the drug store) can be inserted into the appropriate place in the schedule.

The use of visual supports can be easily combined with other teaching methods. For example, when using direct teaching to help Charles learn to push the button on the pop-up toy, it may be helpful to cover up the rest of the toy with a piece of cloth to help him focus on the button without the distraction of the other switches. Or it may be helpful to place a colored sticker on the exact spot he needs to push, to increase the chances that he will be successful and to reduce frustration. Both of these are examples of ways to provide visual clarification of what we want him to do during an adult-directed teaching activity.

Visual supports can also be used during child-directed activities. For example, instead of climbing on the shelves to get the ball she wants to play with, Maria can learn to point to or bring you a picture of the ball from her choice board (discussed further in a moment). When she does, you will give her the ball.

A choice board contains pictures of a few of your child's favorite toys or activities, attached by Velcro to a piece of cardboard. (Clear laminating sheets can be used to protect the picture from sticky hands.) The choice board should be placed in the same area each day and should be within your child's reach. You can change the pictures on the board so that there is some variety in the options available to her, but you should always include at least one of her favorite toys. If you don't want to draw your own pictures or take photographs for visual supports, the Boardmaker software program by Mayer-Johnson (www.mayer-johnson.com) is an excellent resource for simple, clear pictures.

Identifying and Using Rewards

In an earlier chapter, I mentioned that social rewards such as praise may not be sufficiently motivating to children with autism, who don't crave social attention anyway. For example, watching car wheels roll may be much more satisfying for Maria than hearing her mother say "Good job." In that case, it will be very hard to teach her a different way to play with a car if her only reward is verbal praise from her mom. So we need to find ways to motivate children with autism to participate in teaching activities with us so that they can learn new skills.

In addition to social rewards such as attention, other types of rewards (also called reinforcers) can include foods, toys, or activities. The following lists show examples of each.

Food

- Should come in small pieces that can be consumed quickly
- Should be able to be eaten independently and safely
- *Examples:* chips, grapes, popcorn, cereal, raisins, goldfish crackers, pieces of health bar, pretzels

Toys

- Should be something the child enjoys but does not become overly absorbed in or attached to
- Should have a clear end point; otherwise use a timer to indicate the end of the reward period

- *Examples:*

  Vehicles—cars, trucks

  Puzzles (or pieces to be put in the puzzle one at a time)—shapes, letters, numbers, pictures

  Construction toys—blocks, Duplos

  Cause-and-effect toys—jack-in-box, pop-up toy

  Sensory toys—toys with lights, toys that spin, musical toys, Koosh ball

Activities

- Should be developmentally appropriate
- Should have a clear end point; otherwise use a timer to indicate the end of the reward period
- *Examples:*

  Independent—drawing on paper, looking at pictures in books, jumping on a trampoline

  With others—being tickled, being swung around, popping soap bubbles

What is rewarding to one child may not be rewarding to another. One of the best ways to identify motivating rewards is to observe your child carefully. What does he choose to play with when he is alone? What about when he is with others? What are his favorite indoor and outdoor activities? What snacks does he eat most consistently? If he doesn't seem to show much interest in toys, you can present him with different toys and gauge his level of interest by observing whether he looks at it, reaches for it, holds it, or pushes it away.

When you are working with your young child, rewards need to be presented immediately when the child performs the desired response; young children cannot wait. So choose rewards that you can give immediately and that take a short time for the child to use or consume, so that you don't waste valuable teaching time waiting for him or her to finish eating or playing.

It often helps to have the items you are using as rewards available *only* during the teaching activity—that will make them especially powerful. Some children may not find it exciting to get a piece of cereal as a reward if it is the same cereal they eat every morning (or to be allowed to play with a toy that they have free access to during the rest of the day). For other children with more limited interests, these items may work fine as rewards, despite their availability at other times. And remember that something that is rewarding to your child one day may not be rewarding the next. For children whose preferences change, try a "reward box" from which they can choose their one favorite reward of the moment.

Visual supports can be used to illustrate to the child which rewards are available and when they will get them. A choice board (mentioned in the previous section) with two or three pictures of possible rewards can be used to let the child select the reward that he or she wants. A "first-then" board can be used to remind children of the reward they will get after completing an activity. For example, during work sessions at home you can put a picture of the teaching activity that must be completed under the word "First" and a picture of the fun activity or treat the child will get when the activity is over under the word "Then," and teach your child to follow the first-then sequence.

When using rewards to motivate a child with autism, keep in mind these two important teaching suggestions:

1. Always provide *social rewards* along with other types of rewards so that your child learns the value of a smile or a "Great job!"

2. Make sure to reward your child's *attempts and efforts*, as well as his or her successes. You want the teaching process to be as pleasant as possible for your child as he or she moves along the road toward mastery of important skills.

Using Prompts

When presenting activities to your child, you always need to be aware of the delicate line between those that offer the appropriate level of challenge and those that are overly frustrating for the child. No teaching session is fun if we always fail. That's where prompts come in. Prompts are behaviors we use to increase the likelihood that the child will respond correctly. They give children additional information about what they are supposed to do so that they can respond correctly and experience success.

There are lots of different kinds of prompts we can use to supplement verbal instructions. Verbal prompts and modeling prompts are the most commonly used with young children, but neither is especially effective with children with autism. If a child doesn't respond to an instruction, many of us have a natural tendency to repeat the instruction or provide additional instructions. However, this may not be the best prompting strategy for young children with autism, for two reasons: (1) it teaches the child that he or she doesn't have to respond immediately to requests, and (2) additional verbal information may not be helpful for children with limited language understanding.

Modeling or gesturing has similar limitations. For example, if Charles doesn't respond to the instruction to push the button of the pop-up toy, we may point to the button or push it ourselves to provide him with more information about the behavior we expect. These approaches may be very effective in some instances, but may not be so helpful for Charles. First of all, he may not understand the pointing gesture or have the ability to imitate the action demonstrated—thus these prompts will not be effective in helping him respond correctly. Second, he may learn to respond only to the prompt and not to the verbal instruction. (I have worked with some children who have imitated the point instead of providing the desired response.) Another drawback is that gestural and modeling prompts can be difficult to fade (withdraw) if the child becomes dependent on them.

The type of prompt we use most commonly at TRIAD when teaching parents to work with their young children is the physical prompt. Physical prompts involve moving the child's body (gently) to perform the desired response. For Charles, we might put our hand over his to help him push the button. This procedure ensures that he will succeed and will receive his reward. Physical prompting also helps children focus on the end-point behavior rather than on the prompt itself. If possible, physical prompts should be provided from behind the child so that he can clearly see the action required to perform the task. Physical prompts also need to be faded, of course, because our goal is to have Charles push the button independently, without our assistance. Luckily, physical prompts are the easiest type to fade. In Charles's case, to fade the prompt we might reduce the pressure on his hand for some trials, then touch his hand briefly for some trials, until he is able to respond consistently to the verbal instruction alone.

A similar prompting method can be used to encourage Maria's use of the choice board to request the ball. When Maria starts to climb up on the shelf to get the ball, her mother can guide Maria (from behind) to the choice board and place her own hand over Maria's to touch the picture of the ball. Then Maria can have the ball to play with! Maria's mother will gradually withdraw the physical prompts until Maria has learned to use the choice board independently.

In the TRIAD clinic we use these three teaching strategies— combining different teaching methods, identifying and using rewards, and providing prompts—as the foundation for our work with parents. In the following section, you'll see how you can use them when you work on your child's specific areas of need at home.

EVERYDAY TEACHING ACTIVITIES

It's hard work being a parent. We all have busy lives. Maybe you have other children to care for, maybe you have another job outside the home, or maybe you're a single parent without another adult in the home to help get things done. Whatever your situation, I'm guessing that you might be wondering right now, "How can I possibly find the time to teach my child on top of everything else I do?" The answer is surprisingly simple: we need to figure out ways to integrate teaching activities into our everyday routines. We all feed our children, bathe them, and get them dressed. We also spend time playing with them and taking them on outings—maybe they come with us to the park, maybe they accompany us while we are shopping for groceries. These are examples of everyday activities that offer opportunities to teach our children new skills.

Activities to Promote Imitation

Imitation is an important developmental process that begins very early in life. Long before children can walk or talk, they engage in back-and-forth imitation games with adults. Babies often imitate their parent's facial expressions or sounds, and they show enjoyment when their own actions are imitated by adults. These early back-and-forth interactions set the stage for the later development of more complex social and conversational exchanges.

Imitation also provides children with a way to establish interactions with their peers. Some of the earliest interactive games between young children involve imitating each other's actions and switching between being the one who imitates and the one who is imitated. In addition to its social function, imitation also plays an important role in learning. Children learn a variety of skills by observing and imitating the behaviors of their parents, siblings, classmates, and peers.

Research at Vanderbilt and elsewhere has demonstrated that young children with autism are less likely to imitate the actions of others, compared to typically developing children and those with other disorders. The implications of this "imitation impairment" are not entirely clear. However, it is not difficult to see how this impairment might have important consequences for a child's social interactions, communication, and learning. Our own research has shown that children with autism who are better imitators also have better play skills.[1] We have also found that children's imitation skills at age two are predictive of their language skills at age three or four.[2] These results suggest that imitation is an important skill for children with autism to learn. Whereas children without autism begin to imitate others spontaneously and without effort, children with autism often need to be taught imitation skills.

It is often easier for children with autism to learn to imitate actions using objects rather than actions involving body movements, so I would suggest starting your at-home activities using object imitation. To do this, it is helpful to have two sets of materials available, one for you and one for the child. The following list explains the steps to teaching Robbie to imitate banging on a drum with a drumstick.

Step	What to Do	Example
1	Have two sets of materials available.	Clear the floor of the play area and set out a drum and two drumsticks.
2	Get your child's attention.	Say "Look!" or "Watch what I'm doing!"; start to sing a familiar song.
3	As soon as he or she looks in your direction, demonstrate the action, and say "Do this" or "You do it." (Do *not* label the specific action. You want the child to learn to imitate your actions, not follow your verbal instructions.)	When Robbie is looking, hit the drum with your drumstick while saying, "Robbie, do what I do." Continue demonstrating the action to give Robbie a few seconds to respond.
4a	*If the child attempts the imitation*, then provide immediate praise, a reinforcer, or both.	If Robbie beats the drum at least once, reward him by saying, "Great job, Robbie!" giving him a tickle, a small treat, or both.

Step	What to Do	Example
	Demonstrate a different action with the toy and repeat steps 2–4.	Then demonstrate a different action with the drum, such as hitting the side of the drum instead of the top or using your hand instead of the drumstick. Reward all attempts.
4b	*If the child does not imitate your action, then* gently guide him or her to complete the action. After the action has been completed, provide immediate praise, a reinforcer or both. Repeat steps 2–4, gradually reducing the level of prompting over each successive trial. When the child succeeds without prompting, you can change the modeled action, as in 4a.	If Robbie does not imitate, place the drumstick in his hand and physically guide his hand to beat the drum. Then say, "Great job, Robbie!" give him a tickle, a small treat, or both. On subsequent trials, try to reduce the prompts by handing him the stick without guiding his hand, and so on. Reward all attempts.

Another initial approach to teaching imitation to children with autism is to imitate their actions with toys. For example, if Robbie is playing with a drumstick by banging it on the floor, you could sit down near him and start banging the other drumstick on the floor. Watch to see whether he takes notice of your actions. If he does, try demonstrating a different action with the toy, such as banging it on the drum, and see if he will imitate this change.

The following list shows some examples of actions you can model during everyday routines to teach your child to imitate. Siblings can be involved in these activities to serve as additional models. Follow the strategies outlined in the earlier list for teaching your child to imitate the actions you demonstrate.

Routine	Actions to Model
Mealtime	• Stir a spoon in a cup to make chocolate milk.
	• Sprinkle sugar on her cereal, or chocolate chips on his ice cream.
	• Feed a doll with a spoon; feed his baby sister with a spoon.
Bathtime	• Model actions with different water toys that create interesting splashes.
	• Pour water out of a cup to make a waterwheel rotate or to tickle her toes.
	• Use a washcloth to "clean" the face of a plastic animal, his dad's face, or his own arm.
Dressing	• Demonstrate how to raise your arms while putting on (or taking off) her shirt.
	• Brush his hair while you are both looking in a mirror.
	• Show her how you pull off your own shoe or sock.
Playtime	• Model actions with toys that produce interesting sounds or visual effects (such as dropping a ball down a tube to watch it spiral down or putting a shape into a shape sorter to hear the sound it makes).

Activities to Promote Functional Communication

Functional communication includes the ability to communicate with others (1) to make requests and (2) to share interests and experiences (joint attention). Each type of communication can be practiced separately.

Requesting

Some children with autism just don't understand that they can ask for something they want. "It's not that Kyle was being stubborn or difficult," says his dad, Frank. "He really didn't seem to get it that he could ask for help. The kid would climb up on a chair to get a toy that was out of reach even though I was standing right there; he'd cry in frustration when he was hungry without realizing that he could just point to the fridge to get me to open it. I just couldn't get him to let me know what he wanted; it was really frustrating for both of us."

Fortunately, there is a way to teach children with autism how to request the things they want—how to express a preference for milk instead of juice, how to ask for a snack, how to ask for help and for more. And we have found over and over again that as children learn to convey their desires and needs to others, there is often a reduction in those problematic negative behaviors that result from frustration. Activities for each of these different types of requesting are described separately in the next sections. For each activity, keep these four things in mind:

1. Provide visual cues to supplement your language (as explained earlier in the section "Teaching with Visual Supports").

2. Use physical prompting as needed to reduce your child's frustration and ensure his or her success (as explained in "Using Prompts").

3. Provide natural reinforcement during requesting activities. That is, if the child is learning to request a snack, the reward should be the snack, rather than a favorite toy.

4. Reward the child's prompted responses as well as his or her unprompted responses.

Requesting: Making Choices. The opportunities for making choices each day are endless, as Kate, the mother of twenty-two-month-old Ally, knew from frustrating experience. As part of normal give-and-take conversation, Kate would habitually ask Ally such questions as, "What would you like for lunch today, Ally?" Ally wouldn't answer. "Which music tape would you like to hear, Ally?" Ally wouldn't answer. "Do you want to play on the swing or the slide, Ally?" And Ally would still remain silent. Eventually Kate stopped asking and just made all decisions for her daughter.

But giving up won't help Ally learn to communicate her choices; Kate needs to learn more effective strategies for teaching Ally to communicate. There are at least three reasons that Ally might not be responding to Kate's queries: (1) Ally may not understand the language her mother is using (most likely); (2) Ally may not have the verbal skills to respond to her mother's questions (also very likely); (3) Ally may not have a preference for one option over the other. So we need to take all three possibilities into consideration when teaching Ally to make choices.

We do this in three ways: (1) by using visual cues to supplement Kate's language-based request, (2) by requiring a nonverbal (rather than verbal) response from Ally, and (3) by pairing a highly desirable object or activity with an undesirable one to make the choice easy. Following are some examples of alternative ways that Kate could present Ally with the choices described earlier:

Less Effective Strategies	More Effective Strategies
"What would you like for lunch today?"	Kate holds up a jar of peanut butter (a favorite food) in one hand and a broccoli spear (a disliked food) in the other, and asks Ally, "What do you want?" Ally makes a choice by reaching, pointing to, or touching the preferred food. Whichever food she chooses, she gets. (If Ally goofs and reaches for the broccoli, she should get the broccoli, but can then be given the same choice again in a few minutes. Kate can prompt as necessary to get Ally to make the choice that best reflects Ally's preference.)
"Which music tape would you like to hear?"	Kate holds up one music tape in each hand—one is Ally's favorite tape and the other is a tape in which Ally has shown little interest—and asks, "What do you want?"

Less Effective Strategies	More Effective Strategies
	If Ally doesn't make a choice by reaching, pointing to, or touching a tape, Kate can prompt as necessary to get Ally to make the choice that best reflects her preference and then play it immediately.
"Do you want to play on the swing or the slide?"	At the park, Kate presents a choice board to Ally that includes a picture of a swing and a slide, and asks, "What do you want to play on?" If Ally doesn't make a choice by reaching, pointing to, or touching a picture, Kate prompts as necessary to get Ally to make a choice and then takes her to the play area selected.

When you offer a choice to your child, follow these four steps to encourage a correct response:

1. Provide visual cues and say, "What do you want?"
2. Wait five seconds for your child to respond.
3. Prompt as needed to get a reach, touch, or point response to one of the objects or pictures.
4. Provide whichever item your child chooses.

It's helpful to start teaching choice making by presenting two actual objects. As your child begins to understand the concept of choice making and that pictures represent real objects, you can switch to photographs, pictures, or drawings of objects instead. You can also eventually present more than two options at a time by putting three or four cards on a choice board. When starting out, it is good to require the simplest and easiest behavioral response from your child. For most children with autism, reaching and touching are usually much easier responses to teach than pointing.

Requesting: Initiating Spontaneous Requests. When a child makes a choice between objects or activities, he or she is responding to an initiation from an adult. Because the adult initiates the interaction and limits the child's choices, it's often a good way to start teaching the child the communicative process. However, the ultimate goal of communication is for it to be spontaneous. We don't want to have to offer options and wait for a child to respond. We may not know the right options to offer. And we want the child to be active in expressing his desires and needs, for the sake of his own independence and self-determination. So we also need to make sure that the child has a way to initiate requests spontaneously.

When teaching your child to ask for things he or she wants, there are two very important principles to keep in mind:

1. It is critical to capitalize on your child's interests and preferences by using highly motivating objects and activities. Remember, the reward your child gets is the item (or activity) that he or she requests, so if it's not highly desirable, teaching will take a lot longer. Refer back to the lists of possible reinforcers presented earlier in this chapter to identify your child's favorite objects and activities. For example, if your child loves to be swung in the air, then teaching her to request swinging is a great idea. If your child loves chocolate pudding, then that's another good item to teach him to request.

2. To get the child to request spontaneously, you will need to set up situations in which she is highly motivated to request. For example, you might swing your child in the air and then pause and wait for a request before you continue. Or you can give him chocolate pudding without taking the cover off, so that he needs to request your assistance to get this highly desirable item.

There are lots of different approaches to teaching children to request. For example, we can teach the child to request by using words, symbols, objects, pictures, gestures—or a combination of these different methods. We can also teach the child to request each specific object or activity (for example, pudding, swing) or to request a variety of objects or activities using the concepts of "help" or "more." If your child has a speech-language therapist, it's a good idea to check with him or her for recommendations about which approach to take. Whichever approach you decide to use, be sure to keep things simple and teach one thing at a time.

Because most young children with autism have difficulty even at the nonverbal level of communicating, the examples in this section will focus on teaching the child nonverbal methods of requesting. Even though we may not be expecting a verbal response from your child at this point, we still need to model the appropriate use of language for the child. I have decided to focus on teaching "more" and "help" because these general, all-purpose requests can be used in many types of situations. Another important type of communication to teach children early on is how to request a break from an activity or indicate that he or she is "finished" or "all done"; the ability to communicate this message can prevent undesirable behaviors that the child may use instead of communicating his or her need more directly.

The procedures for teaching a child to request "more" and "help" are similar, and follow the same general sequence:

1. Set up a situation in which the child is motivated to obtain a desired object or activity.

2. Wait five seconds for the child to initiate a request using the method selected (such as handing you a card with the appropriate symbol).

3. If the child hands you the card, model the appropriate language (such as, "You want help!" or "You want more chips!") and immediately provide the requested object or activity. If the child does not hand you the card, physically prompt him to give you the card. Model the appropriate language (such as

by saying, "You want help!" or "You want more chips!") and then immediately provide the requested object or activity.

Requesting "More." To teach children to request "more," we have to interrupt activities that they are enjoying so that they will have to communicate with us to get us to resume the activities. Children can be taught to communicate a request for more by making the sign for more, by pointing to a "more" symbol, or by handing us a card that contains a "more" symbol. Of course they can also request the specific object or activity instead of invoking the concept of more. The following are a few simple ideas for setting up situations to motivate children to ask for more:

- Engage your child in a favorite physical activity, such as tickling, jumping, or swinging, and then stop so that he needs to ask for more to continue the game.

- Give him his snack in small portions so that he must ask you for more at fairly frequent intervals.

- Interrupt one of his favorite activities (turn off the music or remove a toy he is playing with) so that he needs to ask you for more.

Requesting Help. To teach children to request help, we need to set up situations in which the child needs our assistance to get something that he or she wants very much. The process is similar to the one used to teach "more." Children can be taught to request help by using the sign for help, by pointing to a "help" symbol, or by handing us a card that contains a "help" symbol. If the child were to request the specific object or activity instead of invoking the concept of help, we would also accept that response. The following are some ways to motivate children to request help:

- Give your child a new toy that she likes that has not yet been removed from its packaging. She will need help removing the packaging to get to the toy.

- Give her a favorite food without removing the wrapper. Granola bars and packaged pudding snacks are examples of foods that many children need help to unwrap.
- Place a favorite toy out of reach so she must ask for your assistance in getting it.
- Withhold part of a toy so that it cannot be completed or operated correctly without the missing part. For example, give her a windup toy without the key to wind it.

There are many daily activities and routines that you can easily use to teach and practice requesting:

Routine	Choice Making	Requesting Help	Requesting "More"
Mealtime	Offer child a choice between two desserts or between two drinks.	Give child a favorite food without removing the wrapper or a juice box without opening it.	Give child a very small portion of a favorite food or drink, and place more within his view.
Bathtime	Offer child a choice of bath toys to play with.	Hand child a favorite bath toy that she cannot operate herself.	Pause in the middle of child's favorite bath routine (for example, pouring water on his feet).
Playtime	Offer child a choice of toys to play with, music to listen to, or tapes to watch.	Put a favorite toy out of child's reach but within his view.	Pause in the middle of a swinging game or other favorite activity of child.

Joint Attention

Joint attention is a term used to describe the ability to shift visual attention between another person and an object or event of interest. When children *respond* to joint attention, they follow another person's focus of attention. For example, Johnny's father sees something interesting across the street and says, "Look over there! That dog is wearing a hat!" as he points to the dog. Johnny's eighteen-month-old brother stops in his tracks, looks at the dog, and looks back at his father and laughs. But thirty-three-month-old Johnny doesn't look up or respond. It's almost as if he doesn't hear his dad's excited voice.

When children *initiate* joint attention, they are trying to get someone else to pay attention to something they're interested in. For example, Johnny's brother initiates joint attention by walking over to his father to show him a piece of artwork he has created or by pointing to a spider building a web outside the window; he then looks back at his father to make sure he is paying attention. Children initiate joint attention for purely social purposes: to share an interest or experience. Johnny's father can't think of a single time that Johnny has tried to communicate with him to share his interest.

Children with autism often have difficulty initiating and responding to joint attention. They may be less likely to look in the direction that others are looking or to look in the direction that another person is pointing. Because they are not sharing this visual information with adults, they may have fewer opportunities to learn from others about the objects and events in their environment. The same is true for initiating joint attention; when a child points to or shows objects to an adult, the adult often responds by talking to and paying attention to the child. Because these are behaviors that can foster language development, children who do not initiate joint attention have fewer opportunities to obtain language input from adults.

Responding to joint attention can be taught more readily than *initiating* joint attention in young children with autism, so it's best to start your at-home exercises with activities like those described here, which stress responding. These activities address two component skills of responding to joint attention: (1) looking back and forth between an adult and an object (or event) and (2) understanding gestures as a source of information.

To encourage your child to shift his or her gaze between an object and a person:

- Model exaggerated verbal and facial responses to "surprise" events. When unexpected or surprising events occur during the course of the day (the doorbell rings, a block tower falls over, the dog barks), look at your child, make an exaggerated look of surprise (raise your eyebrows, smile and open your mouth wide, make a gasping sound, cover your mouth with your hand), and say enthusiastically, "Wow!" or "Uh-oh!" Your tone should be positive. Watch for your child's response. If your child looks at you, you can reward him by saying, "Good looking!" or by giving her a brief tickle. If your child doesn't look at you, keep trying this during different parts of the day.

- Set up play activities so that a surprise event occurs periodically. For example, gasp and cover your mouth when the child activates a jack-in-the-box, or say "Hello" every time the child opens a door on a pop-up toy and "Good-bye" every time he or she closes it. Once the routine is established, pause before responding to see if the child looks at you expectantly, and give lots of praise if he or she does.

To help your child learn that gestures are a source of information:

- Throughout the day, in different settings, try to direct your child's attention to interesting events or favorite objects by pointing in their direction and saying "Look!" in an excited tone of voice. Begin by pointing at objects that are very close to your extended finger; gradually increase the distance between your finger and the object. When possible, give the child the object after he or she follows the point.

- Gather some of your child's favorite toys or objects (parts of a puzzle, balls that go down a chute, cars that go on a track) and place them in different parts of the room. When starting this activity, the objects should be fairly close to the child and at least partially visible. Start playing a game with her so that she needs the objects you've hidden. When the need becomes apparent, shrug your shoulders and say, "Hmm, where is it?" Then point to the object and say, "There it is!" When your child is able to find the objects consistently, try turning your head in the direction of the object instead of pointing to it. Eventually you can try just shifting your eyes to indicate the general direction of the object. Be sure to use objects that are highly motivating for your child.

Activities to Promote Interactive Play

As we have discussed, difficulty with social interactions is a core deficit for children with autism. Following is a list of early social interaction skills that develop through the preschool years. Children with typical development often acquire these skills naturally, through their everyday experiences, but children with autism often require explicit instruction to learn even the most basic of these skills. This list may be helpful to you in determining your child's IFSP (or IEP) goals, to ensure that this critical area of development is addressed in your child's intervention program.

Early Social Interaction Skills

- Attends to adults
- Imitates the actions of adults
- Responds to the social bids of adults
- Initiates social interactions with adults
- Plays simple interaction and turn-taking games with adults
- Plays in the proximity of peers
- Attends to the activities of peers
- Imitates the actions of peers

- Responds to initiations from peers
- Initiates interactions with peers
- Shares materials with peers (for example, relinquishes materials on request; requests materials from peers appropriately)
- Plays turn-taking games with peers (for example, throws a basketball into a hoop)
- Engages in cooperative, goal-directed activities with peers (for example, constructs a building with blocks)

This section will focus primarily on teaching turn-taking interactions because this is a foundation skill for developing social understanding and communicative exchanges. You can see from the preceding list that imitation is an important type of social interaction, so the imitation activities presented earlier (in the section "Activities to Promote Imitation") can also be used to develop interactive play.

However, there are some important differences between imitation and interactive play. Relative to imitation, interactive play (1) extends over *several* back-and-forth turns and (2) requires that the child recognize the partner's turn and actively direct a behavior toward the partner to keep the interaction going. The key element to interactive play is the turn-taking aspect of the interaction; the child does not necessarily need to imitate the same action with the toy.

The following steps can be used to teach turn-taking play:

Step	What to Do	Example
1	Sit across from the child, get his attention, and perform an action with a toy as he watches.	Select a puzzle that Micah enjoys and is able to complete independently. Sit across from him with the puzzle in front of you. Scatter the pieces so that some are near you and some are near Micah. Say "Look Micah" and put a puzzle piece into the puzzle as he watches.

Step	What to Do	Example
2	Indicate that it is the child's turn by pushing the toy toward him and saying "Your turn!"	Push the puzzle toward Micah and say "Your turn!" If necessary, prompt him by handing him a puzzle piece.
3	After about fifteen seconds, whether or not the child engages with the toy, say "My turn!" as you pat your chest.	Whether or not Micah puts in a piece, say "My turn!" as you pat your chest, and encourage him to pass the puzzle back to you.
4a	*If the child pushes the toy back,* provide praise and repeat steps 1–3.	If Micah pushes the toy back, say "Thanks Micah!" or "Good job!" enthusiastically and repeat the sequence until the puzzle is completed.
4b	*If the child doesn't push the toy back,* physically guide* him to do so and provide praise. Repeat steps 1–3.	If Micah doesn't push the toy back, extend your hand in a requesting gesture. If he still does not pass it back, physically guide* him to do so. Say "My turn!" and repeat steps 1–3.

*Note: If possible, it is best if another person can guide him from behind.

The activities described here will focus on teaching turn taking with you, but these activities can be adapted easily to include siblings, peers, or other family members:

- Make a game out of rolling a toy truck (or ball) back and forth. Create a routine in which you vocalize before rolling it to the child and express excitement when you get it back. Provide prompting as needed to get the child to roll the truck back. Alter the game by making the vocalization and then pausing before rolling the truck, by rolling him a different truck, or by having the truck jump over an obstacle before rolling it. Keep the game interesting by rolling three trucks to him at once, by putting a piece of candy in the truck, or by having the truck knock over a stack of blocks. Model enjoyment by exaggerating your facial expressions and gestures. For example, throw your arms in the air dramatically as you gasp and make a surprised face during this game.

- Develop turn-taking games that involve passing some of your child's favorite toys back and forth. For example, you can put the pieces of a shape sorter (or puzzle) on the floor and then pass the shape sorter back and forth to each other as you each take a turn putting a shape in. Other games might include taking turns dropping balls down a tube, throwing balls into a basket, or rolling cars down a graded track. As you pass the toy back and forth, you can use the cues "my turn" and "your turn" to increase her understanding of the game.

- Develop play routines with finger songs or physical games that your child likes and that require some response from him or her. For example, pause while singing a familiar song and wait for your child to look at you (or take your hand or say something) before continuing.

The following are some examples for integrating turn-taking activities into everyday routines:

Routine	Turn-Taking Activity
Mealtime	• Have family members take turns taking a cookie off a plate and then passing the plate to the person next to them.
Bathtime	• Take turns with your child filling a cup with water and pouring it onto a waterwheel.
	• Take turns operating a bath toy.
Dressing	• Take turns with your child pulling each other's socks off, little by little.

- Put a silly hat on your own head (or your child's) and pass it back and forth as you take turns with each other putting it on.

When a child with autism develops improved interaction skills, the whole family benefits. Parents feel more connected to their child and better able to participate in community activities, and siblings have the opportunity to engage with the brother or sister who had previously been inaccessible.

Activities to Promote Functional Play Skills with Toys

The birthday party was in full swing. Six little two-year-olds along with their younger and older siblings ran around the backyard breaking in the birthday boy's new toys. Some children pretended they were NFL linebackers as they ran for a touchdown with the foam football. Others blew bubbles and chased them around, hoping to pop them all. Still another group was gathered waiting a turn to play with the mechanical dog that jumped and barked just like a real dog. But the birthday boy himself, two-year-old James, sat alone at the picnic table staring at the ribbons that had adorned the packages. His mom and dad encouraged him to play with his birthday gifts, but they didn't insist, knowing that pulling James away from the ribbons could lead to a temper tantrum that would ruin the party. James, they knew, had autism.

Children without autism just know how to play. It's a skill that they pick up by watching others, by listening to instructions, and by using their imaginations. Young children with autism, however, have trouble imitating, understanding language, and imagining, so they need someone to teach them how to play. Play skills are valuable to a child because they increase the child's opportunities for peer interactions and for learning new skills.

Functional play is the skill of using toys the way they are intended. For example, toy cars are manufactured so that children can run them along imaginary roads and take play people from one place to another. Functional play acts also include putting a bottle to a doll's mouth, looking at a book and turning the pages, placing a cup on a saucer, building with blocks, and pressing buttons on a toy cash register. More complex functional acts involve sequences of actions with toys, such as giving a doll a bottle and then putting it to sleep, or pressing the buttons on a toy cash register, taking out some coins, putting the coins in the back of a toy truck, and driving the truck to the store. A child with autism, however, may be more likely to play with toys such as cars by spinning their wheels or lining them up in a row.

The process of teaching functional play skills is very similar to that described for teaching imitation: you need to demonstrate appropriate actions with toys. The one difference has to do with what and how you model. When teaching imitation, you don't label the action because you want the child to learn to watch you to find out what to do. In contrast, when you are teaching functional play, it's a good idea to model simple language to describe what you're doing and why. Young children with autism have particular difficulty playing with stuffed animals or dolls and creating play sequences, so the activities here focus on these skills:

- Teach your child to play functionally with a teddy bear or doll. Get two teddy bears (or dolls) and give one to your child and keep one for yourself. Model an action with your own bear; actions can include feeding it, having it drive a car, having it sneeze, having it walk over to a chair to sit down, and so on. Label the action as you do it ("Look—the bear is driving a car!"). Encourage your child to imitate the same action with his bear. Make the actions and accompanying sounds interesting and dramatic to attract your child's attention. You might, for example, make the teddy bear sneeze with a great big buildup in a funny deep bear voice and then explode with a gigantic sneeze that knocks the bear right off his feet.

- You can help your child see that play involves sequential acts by combining several small actions. You might have the teddy bear give his big sneeze and then you can wipe his nose with a tissue; you might first stir a spoon in a cup and then give the doll a drink from the cup; you might put little people in a toy truck, push the truck to the other side of the room, then take the little people out of the truck. Again, label your activities (for example, "We're stirring tea for the doll—look, she likes it, she's drinking it all up—glug, glug, glug.").

Whichever skills you choose to work on, keep these tips in mind:

1. Timing is everything. You want to make these activities fun for your child. If she is showing signs of being tired, stop. Don't try to do too much at once.
2. Don't worry if you don't see immediate results. Every small improvement is important. It may be more important that your child is *watching* your activity than that he is imitating your actions.
3. You don't have to be your child's teacher 24/7. Give yourself (and your child) breaks. You both need it.
4. Remember to use prompting to decrease your child's frustration. If an activity seems to be too hard for her, it's fine to back down to an easier one so that she experiences success.

A STORY OF EARLY DETECTION: PART FOUR

Luke's mother, Judy, continues their story.

I'm really happy with Luke's therapists, but I don't feel comfortable leaving the intervention to other people—I feel like we have to work with Luke at home too. I picked up some ideas from watching his therapy sessions and also from all the reading I've been doing, but I found it very difficult to actually implement the activities on my own. What really helped the most was having one of his therapists show me exactly what to do and let me try it while she watched and coached me. Not only did that help me feel like I knew what I was doing, but it also helped me teach Jeff what I had learned.

Luke has made great strides since he started all of his therapies, and working with him at home myself has helped me understand him better and feel more confident in my parenting skills. I had always considered myself a good parent, but having a child with autism seems to present some unique challenges that I had never before imagined.

One of the strategies that has worked the best for us is using visual structure. Luke is a very visual child, and he learned to follow a picture schedule pretty quickly. With the schedule, I could show him when he would get to play on the trampoline and play with his cars. It seemed to calm him down when he saw that the pictures were there. Something else that worked really well for us was a Time Timer, which shows Luke how much more time he has left in different activities. We also use a "finished box" to help him transition between activities. When one activity is finished, he puts his materials in the box and is ready for the next one.

Luke is communicating with us more often at home too—he seems to be less frustrated as he gets better at letting us know what he wants. Right now he uses a combination of words, signs, and pictures. He still doesn't look at us as much as we'd like him to, but I feel hopeful that that will come with time. He's learned how to play better with toys, and sometimes when the neighborhood kids come by to play with him I see him watch them and copy what they do. Boy is that a change! So far I am very pleased with how Luke is progressing. I know we still have a way to go, but each day I feel more optimistic that he will be able to attend a regular kindergarten class with his neighborhood pals.

FREQUENTLY ASKED QUESTIONS

I work hard with my daughter at home, but I'm starting to think it's all a waste of time. When we finally make a breakthrough, she seems to forget the new skill the next day. Yesterday, for example, she imitated the way I was playing with her doll, giving me such hope; when I tried the game again today, she acted as if she had no idea what I wanted her to do. How do I know she's getting any benefit from the time I put in at home working on these activities?

I know how hard it can be to wait for your child to show the changes you want so desperately to see. But it's important to keep in mind that change doesn't come all at once. And sometimes we forget how far our children have come. For example, even if your child doesn't imitate your actions one day, is she better at sitting down with you than she used to be? Is she watching your actions more than she used to? Does she have more interest in the doll than she did before you started working with her? Do you understand what drives her behavior more than you did before? My guess is that if you have been working with her for a few weeks, the answer to at least some of these questions is yes. So take a deep breath and pay attention to the small changes that you see, because they are the building blocks that enable the bigger changes to occur!

My son is receiving therapy twice a week through the state EI program. He works with a speech-language pathologist and a special education teacher. They both say he is doing very well and showing much improvement, but I don't see it at home at all. How can I help him transfer the things he learns with his teachers to his daily activities outside the clinic?

Children with autism don't generalize their skills to different settings as well as other children, so it's not surprising to hear that he's doing things in the therapy session that he's not doing at home. But that just means that his teachers need to add generalization as a goal. There are several ways to help children with autism generalize their skills. One is for you to observe the therapy sessions so you can see the types of activities they are doing and the approaches they are using. That may help you use similar methods at home. You should also ask his therapists to give you specific suggestions for helping him transfer his skills to the home setting. Maybe they can write up a home program of specific activities you can do with him. Maybe they will come do some sessions with him at your home. Maybe you can be part of his sessions, and the therapists can teach you some ways to work with him at home. It may be helpful to raise your concerns with your EI service coordinator, in case your child's IFSP needs to be changed to incorporate generalization as a new goal.

When you work with your child at home, whether in a structured teaching program or in a casual program using daily activities, you are giving your child not only a better chance of improving his or her developmental skills but also your time, attention, and love. Those three things are desperately needed by all children, but perhaps especially by children with autism, who are sometimes so distant and "different" that they can be hard to understand and get close to. It may seem as though your child wants to be left alone, but that's only because he or she doesn't know how to communicate or interact the way other children do. So use the suggestions in this chapter to improve those deficits that are so common in children with autism, but also to better know your child—the unique and wonderful human being that he or she truly is.

EPILOGUE

The journey parents make from their first suspicion of autism to the official diagnosis of the disorder can be a long and emotionally tiring one. It is my hope that this book will ease the way. But even with my advice and suggestions to guide you, the big questions in the autism arena still remain unanswered: What causes autism, and how can it best be treated? The desire to answer these questions is what drives my days as a researcher, and I hope that by the time I prepare a revised edition of this book, we will have greater scientific knowledge about the puzzle that is autism.

But for now, at the end of a book like this, I feel that I should offer some kind of sage advice to those parents who find themselves newly immersed in this complex disorder. So I've struggled with various words of wisdom, jotting some down for review and tossing others in the mental wastebasket before they are even fully formed. What can I say to help you move forward? What words do I have that will give you the courage and strength you'll need in the months and years ahead?

Then I realized that my words are not at all what you need as you look toward the future. So I quickly sent out a request through our TRIAD research newsletter asking parents of children with autism what advice they would give to parents just entering this world. They are the ones who truly understand what you're feeling.

They have been where you are today. So I end this book with their words of support and wisdom:

> Let your child's safe haven be at home. He or she will have enough to deal with in the world. Home needs to be a place of shelter, where there's no yelling or violence. Patience is the key. Never ever yell at your autistic child. Also, be an advocate for your child. If the parents don't advocate for their child, who will? (mother of four-year-old boy)

> The one thing I would like to tell parents who are worried that their young child is not developing as he should is that your child is still your unique little person that you have grown to love. Get the child tested, give him or her every opportunity to learn, and then try to join him in his world as much as possible to help draw him into your world. (mother of five-year-old boy)

> Don't delay in getting your child diagnosed. It may not be autism, but if it is, the sooner you start getting help the better. And remember that the way she behaves is NOT her fault. (father of three-year-old girl)

> Become educated about autism so you can understand and help your child. Work with your school and teacher to continue practicing skills at home. Set your own goals for your child and work together to help your child achieve those goals. (mother of three-and-a-half-year-old boy)

> All of us need and want love. And a child with autism is no different. Love your child through all of his trials and celebrations. Praise him for all of his efforts, whether he fails or accomplishes his goal. Staying positive will uplift your child's spirit and give him self-confidence throughout his journey. (mother of eight-year-old boy)

The best advice I can give the parents of a child with autism is to look at your child as a unique little person who has many challenges *and* gifts. Try to help him overcome the challenges and apply the gifts by joining him in his world; you may find that the more you join him in his world, the more he will come out and play in yours! (father of three-year-old girl)

The best piece of advice I can give to parents of a young child with autism is what the angels said to the shepherds: "Be not afraid." Empower yourself with knowledge. Don't be afraid of the word *autism*. Don't be afraid of the therapies; don't be afraid of the doctors and professionals; don't be afraid of the schools or teachers; and don't be afraid of your own instincts. Fear will make you overreact or underreact, and neither is good for your child. (mother of five-year-old boy)

I'd like to let parents know that autism is not caused by anything they did and that their child is not to blame either. It's okay to feel depressed, but don't let the guilt and anxiety destroy your relationship with your child, your other children, or your spouse. This is a time to get closer, not further apart. (mother of six-year-old boy)

❧

There you have it. Just a few words of support and encouragement from other parents who know exactly how you feel. This kind of support will be important for you and your child as you explore the answer to the question: "Does my child have autism?"

DIAGNOSTIC CRITERIA FOR AUTISTIC DISORDER

A. A total of six (or more) items from (1), (2), and (3), with at least two from (1) and one each from (2) and (3):
   (1) qualitative impairment in social interaction, as manifested by at least two of the following:
      (a) marked impairment in the use of multiple nonverbal behaviors such as eye-to-eye gaze, facial expression, body postures, and gestures to regulate social interaction
      (b) failure to develop peer relationships appropriate to developmental level
      (c) lack of spontaneous seeking to share enjoyment, interests, or achievements with other people (e.g., by lack of showing, bringing, or pointing out objects of interest)
      (d) lack of social or emotional reciprocity
   (2) qualitative impairments in communication, as manifested by at least one of the following:
      (a) delay in, or total lack of, the development of spoken language (not accompanied by an attempt to compensate through alternative modes of communication such as gesture or mime)

Reprinted with permission from the *Diagnostic and Statistical Manual of Mental Disorders, Fourth Edition, Text Revision* (Copyright 2000). American Psychiatric Association.

      (b) in individuals with adequate speech, marked impairment in the ability to initiate or sustain a conversation with others

      (c) stereotyped and repetitive use of language or idiosyncratic language

      (d) lack of varied, spontaneous make-believe play or social imitative play appropriate to developmental level

  (3) restricted repetitive and stereotyped patterns of behavior, interests, and activities, as manifested by at least one of the following:

      (a) encompassing preoccupation with one or more stereotyped and restricted patterns of interest that is abnormal either in intensity or focus

      (b) apparently inflexible adherence to specific, nonfunctional routines or rituals

      (c) stereotyped and repetitive motor mannerisms (e.g., hand or finger flapping or twisting, or complex whole-body movements)

      (d) persistent preoccupation with parts of objects

B. Delays or abnormal functioning in at least one of the following areas, with onset prior to age 3 years:

  (1) social interaction,

  (2) language as used in social communication, or

  (3) symbolic or imaginative play

C. The disturbance is not better accounted for by Rett's Disorder or Childhood Disintegrative Disorder.

MODIFIED CHECKLIST FOR AUTISM IN TODDLERS (M-CHAT)

Please fill out the following about how your child **usually** is. Please try to answer every question. If the behavior is rare (e.g., you've seen it once or twice), please answer as if the child does not do it.

1. Does your child enjoy being swung, bounced on your knee, etc.?   Yes   No

2. Does your child take an interest in other children?   Yes   No

3. Does your child like climbing on things, such as up stairs?   Yes   No

4. Does your child enjoy playing peek-a-boo/ hide-and-seek?   Yes   No

5. Does your child ever pretend, for example, to talk on the phone or take care of dolls, or pretend other things?   Yes   No

6. Does your child ever use his/her index finger to point, to ask for something?   Yes   No

7. Does your child ever use his/her index finger to point, to indicate interest in something?   Yes   No

8. Can your child play properly with small toys (e.g., cars or bricks) without just mouthing, fiddling, or dropping them?   Yes   No

9. Does your child ever bring objects over to you (parent) to show you something?   Yes   No

10. Does your child look you in the eye for more than a second or two?   Yes   No

11. Does your child ever seem oversensitive to noise (e.g., plugging ears)?   Yes   No

12. Does your child smile in response to your face or your smile?   Yes   No

13. Does your child imitate you (e.g., you make a face—will your child imitate it)?   Yes   No

14. Does your child respond to his/her name when you call?   Yes   No

15. If you point at a toy across the room, does your child look at it?   Yes   No

16. Does your child walk?   Yes   No

17. Does your child look at things you are looking at?   Yes   No

18. Does your child make unusual finger movements near his/her face?   Yes   No

19. Does your child try to attract your attention to his/her own activity?   Yes   No

20. Have you ever wondered if your child is deaf?   Yes   No

21. Does your child understand what people say?   Yes   No

22. Does your child sometimes stare at nothing or wander with no purpose?   Yes   No

23. Does your child look at your face to check
your reaction when faced with something
unfamiliar?   Yes   No

Scoring the M-CHAT

1. Compare your answers to each item with those listed in the key below.

2. Add up the total number of items that match (out of the 23 items): ____

3. Add up the number of items that match the 6 answers below with asterisks: ____

1. no	*13. no
*2. no	*14. no
3. no	*15. no
4. no	16. no
5. no	17. no
6. no	18. yes
*7. no	19. no
8. no	20. yes
*9. no	21. no
10. no	22. yes
11. yes	23. no
12. no	

Interpreting the M-CHAT

Your child's score is in the "at risk" category if *either* of the following conditions is met:

1. The total number of matching items (out of 23) is 3 or higher, *or*

2. The number of items with asterisks that match (out of 6) is 2 or higher.

Note: An "at risk" score suggests the need for further evaluation, but does not mean that your child has autism (see Chapter Three).

NOTES

CHAPTER ONE

1. Autism Society of America. "What Is Autism?" www.Autism-society. org, 2005. (To access article, click on "Understanding Autism.")

CHAPTER TWO

1. Metropolitan Atlanta Developmental Disabilities Surveillance Program. "Developmental Disabilities." www.cdc.gov/ncbddd/dd/ ddsurv.htm#prev, 2005.

2. Zwaigenbaum, L., and others. "Behavioral Manifestations of Autism in the First Year of Life." *International Journal of Developmental Neuroscience*, 2005, *23*, 143–152.

CHAPTER THREE

1. Filipek, P. A., and others. "Practice Parameter: Screening and Diagnosis of Autism: Report of the Quality Standards Subcommittee of the American Academy of Neurology and the Child Neurology Society." *Neurology*, 2000, *55*, 468–479.

2. Robins, D., Fein, D., Barton, M., and Green, J. "The Modified Checklist for Autism in Toddlers: An Initial Study Investigating the Early Detection of Autism and Pervasive Developmental

Disorders." *Journal of Autism and Developmental Disorders*, 2001, *31*(2), 131–144.

3. Howlin, P., and Moore, A. "Diagnosis of Autism: A Survey of Over 1200 Patients in the UK." *Autism,* 1997, *1,* 135–162.

4. Stone, W. L., Coonrod, E. E., Pozdol, S. L., and Turner, L. M. "The Parent Interview for Autism-Clinical Version (PIA-CV): A Measure of Behavioral Change for Young Children with Autism." *Autism,* 2003, *7,* 9–30.

   Stone, W. L., and Hogan, K. L. "A Structured Parent Interview for Identifying Young Children with Autism." *Journal of Autism and Developmental Disorders*, 1993, *23,* 639–652.

5. Lord, C., Rutter, M., and LeCouteur, A. "Autism Diagnostic Interview-Revised: A Revised Version of a Diagnostic Interview for Caregivers of Individuals with Possible Pervasive Developmental Disorders." *Journal of Autism and Developmental Disorders*, 1994, *24,* 659–685.

6. Sparrow, S., Balla, D., and Cicchetti, D. *Vineland Adaptive Behavior Scales.* Circle Pines, Minn.: American Guidance Service, 1984.

7. Bayley, N. *The Bayley Scales of Infant Development.* (2nd ed.) San Antonio, Tex.: Harcourt Assessment, 1993.

8. Mullen, E. M. *Mullen Scales of Early Learning.* Circle Pines, Minn.: American Guidance Service, 1995.

9. Courchesne, E., Carper, R., and Akshoomoff, N. "Evidence of Brain Overgrowth in the First Year of Life in Autism." *Journal of the American Medical Association,* 2003, *290,* 337–344.

10. Lord, C., and others. "The Autism Diagnostic Observation Schedule-Generic: A Standard Measure of Social and Communication Deficits Associated with the Spectrum of Autism." *Journal of Autism and Developmental Disorders*, 2000, *30,* 205–223.

11. Schopler, E., Reicher, R. J., and Renner, B. R. *The Childhood Autism Rating Scale.* New York: Irvington, 1986.

CHAPTER FOUR

1. Committee on Educational Interventions for Children with Autism. *Educating Children with Autism*. Washington, D.C.: National Academy Press, 2001.

   Dawson, G., and Osterling, J. "Early Intervention in Autism." In M. J. Guralnick (ed.), *The Effectiveness of Early Intervention* (pp. 307–326). Baltimore: Brookes, 1997.

   Hurth, J., and others. "Areas of Agreement About Effective Practices Among Programs Serving Young Children with Autism Spectrum Disorders." *Infants and Young Children*, 1999, *12*, 17–26.

   New York State Department of Health Early Intervention Program. "Autism/Pervasive Developmental Disorders: Assessment and Intervention for Young Children (Age 0–3 Years)." *Clinical Practice Guideline: Autism/Pervasive Developmental Disorders*. New York: New York State Department of Health, 1999.

   Strain, P. S., Wolery, M., and Izeman, S. "Considerations for Administrators in the Design of Service Options for Young Children with Autism and Their Families." *Young Exceptional Children*, 1998, Winter, pp. 8–16.

2. Individuals with Disabilities Education Act Data. "Number of Children Served Under IDEA by Disability and Age Group." www.ideadata.org/tables27th/ar_aa9.htm, 2003.

3. Stone, W. L., and Yoder, P. J. "Predicting Spoken Language Level in Children with Autism Spectrum Disorders." *Autism*, 2001, *5*, 341–361.

4. Levy, S. E., and others. "Use of Complementary and Alternative Medicine Among Children Recently Diagnosed with Autistic Spectrum Disorder." *Journal of Developmental and Behavioral Pediatrics*, 2003, *24*, 418–423.

   Nickel, R. E. "Controversial Therapies for Young Children with Developmental Disabilities." *Infants and Young Children*, 1996, *8*, 29–40.

5. Lonigan, C. J., Elbert, J. C., and Johnson, S. B. "Empirically Supported Psychosocial Interventions for Children: An Overview." *Journal of Clinical Child Psychology*, 1998, *27*, 138–145.

6. Autism Society of America. *Guidelines for Theory and Practice*. Bethesda, Md.: Autism Society of America, 1997.

   Freeman, B. J. "Guidelines for Evaluating Intervention Programs for Children with Autism." *Journal of Autism and Developmental Disorders*, 1997, *27*, 641–651.

   Nickel, R. E. "Controversial Therapies for Young Children with Developmental Disabilities." *Infants and Young Children*, 1996, *8*, 29–40.

7. National Center for Complementary and Alternative Medicine. "10 Things to Know About Evaluating Medical Resources on the Web." NCCAM Publication No. D142. nccam.nih.gov/health/webresources/index.htm, Feb. 19, 2002.

CHAPTER FIVE

1. Stone, W. L., Ousley, O. Y., and Littleford, C. L. "Motor Imitation in Young Children with Autism: What's the Object?" *Journal of Abnormal Child Psychology*, 1997, *25*, 475–485.

2. Stone, W. L., and Yoder, P. J. "Predicting Spoken Language Level in Children with Autism Spectrum Disorders." *Autism*, 2001, *5*, 341–361.

RESOURCES

INTERNET RESOURCES FOR FURTHER INFORMATION ABOUT AUTISM

Additional information about autism is available on the Web sites of federal agencies, professional organizations, and parent organizations. Listed below is a sampling of Web sites that offer informational materials, research opportunities, and resource directories that may be of interest to you.

Federal Agencies and Government-Sponsored Sites

Centers for Disease Control and Prevention (CDC)
www.cdc.gov/ncbddd/autism
This Web site of the CDC's National Center on Birth Defects and Developmental Disabilities features general autism resources, including an information center, an overview on developmental screening, and links to specific CDC programs related to autism.

National Early Childhood Technical Assistance Center (NECTAC)
www.nectas.unc.edu/topics/autism/autism/asp
This Web site provides information and links on early diagnosis, resources, and federally funded projects on autism.

National Dissemination Center for Children with Disabilities (NICHCY)

www.nichcy.org/resources/autism.asp

This Web site contains information specific to autism as well as more general information related to educating children with disabilities.

National Institutes of Health (NIH)

Several different institutes and centers within NIH provide useful information about autism:

- National Institute of Child Health and Human Development (NICHD)

  Autism facts:
  www.nichd.nih.gov/publications/pubs/autism/facts/index.htm
  Autism site: www.nichd.nih.gov/autism/

- National Institute of Deafness and Communication Disorders (NIDCD): www.nidcd.nih.gov/health/voice/autism.asp

- National Institute of Neurological Disorders and Stroke (NINDS): www.ninds.nih.gov/disorders/autism/ autism.htm

- National Institute of Mental Health (NIMH)
  www.nimh.nih.gov/publicat/autism.cfm

National Center for Complementary and Alternative Medicine (NCCAM)

www.nccam.nih.gov

Professional Organizations

The American Academy of Pediatrics (AAP)

www.aap.org/healthtopics/autism.cfm

This Web site provides information about autism detection and treatment. A more general guide to developmental stages that covers children's health topics, including autism, can be found at: www.aap.org/healthtopics/Stages.cfm.

American Speech-Language-Hearing Association (ASHA)

www.asha.org (Go to "most frequent searches" and type in "autism.")

This Web site offers information about autism and the role of the speech-language pathologist.

Parent Organizations

Autism Society of America (ASA)

www.autism-society.org

The ASA offers a wide range of information on topics such as advocacy, education, services, research, and support. The ASA Web site includes Autismsource.org, which is a nationwide online directory of ASA chapters, professionals, government resources, diagnostic centers, and service providers.

National Alliance for Autism Research (NAAR)

www.naar.org

NAAR funds and promotes biomedical research on the causes, prevention, and effective treatment for autism. This site provides general information about autism as well as updates about their research and advocacy efforts.

Cure Autism Now (CAN)

www.cureautismnow.org

CAN supports biomedical research, provides advocacy, and offers a resource network. This site provides general information about autism as well as a resource database and a description of research initiatives.

Organization for Autism Research (OAR)

www.researchautism.org

OAR sponsors research on applied science designed to answer questions that other parents, families, individuals with autism, teachers, and caregivers confront daily. The site includes "A Parent's Guide to Research," to help parents of newly diagnosed children.

First Signs

www.Firstsigns.org

First Signs is dedicated to educating parents and pediatric professionals about the early warning signs of autism and other developmental disorders. This site provides information to promote awareness about the social, emotional, and communication features of autism in young children.

PDD Support Network

www.autism-pdd.net

This information and resource site provides online support and a place for parents to express thoughts, share ideas, and seek help.

ABOUT THE AUTHORS

Wendy L. Stone, Ph.D., is a professor of pediatrics and psychology and human development at Vanderbilt University, director of the Treatment and Research Institute for Autism Spectrum Disorders (TRIAD) at the Vanderbilt Kennedy Center, and co-director of the Marino Autism Research Institute, a collaboration between Vanderbilt University and the University of Miami. She received her doctorate in clinical psychology from the University of Miami in 1981, and completed her internship training at the University of North Carolina and Division TEACCH.

Dr. Stone's primary research interests are in early identification and early intervention for children with Autism Spectrum Disorders. Much of her work has focused on identifying and characterizing the early emerging behavioral features of autism, and she has received federal funding for this research since 1993. She has studied several aspects of early social-communicative development, including play, motor imitation, and prelinguistic communication, examining their contributions to later behavioral and diagnostic outcomes. Her research with young children led to the development of the Screening Tool for Autism in Two-Year-Olds (STAT), which is now being adapted for use with younger children. Current research projects include the identification of social-communicative markers in children under twenty-four months, the prediction of responsiveness to early intervention, and the early social development of later-born siblings of children with autism.

Theresa Foy DiGeronimo, M.Ed., is an award-winning author of many successful books, including *How to Talk to Teens About Really Important Things* and other titles in the Jossey-Bass How to Talk series. She is an adjunct professor of English at William Paterson University in New Jersey.

Index